THE ESOTERIC BACKGROUND
OF WALDORF EDUCATION
The Cosmic Christ Impulse

THE ESOTERIC BACKGROUND OF WALDORF EDUCATION
The Cosmic Christ Impulse

René M. Querido

Rudolf Steiner College Press
Fair Oaks, California

Front cover: photograph by Ted Mahle of "Le Christ Enseignant"
(13th c.), South Portal of the Cathedral of Chartres, France.

Rudolf Steiner College Press
9200 Fair Oaks Boulevard
Fair Oaks, California 95628
© 1995 by René M. Querido
Printed in the United States of America.

ISBN 0-945803-25-7

To present and future Waldorf teachers, to parents and friends seeking to discover the deeper aspects of Waldorf education as Rudolf Steiner conceived of them during the founding years (1919–1925), and to the subsequent development of the Waldorf movement all over the world.

Acknowledgements

I would like to express my gratitude to the Council of the Pedagogical Section in America for having invited me to give a series of five lectures on this theme on the occasion of the Annual Waldorf Teachers' Conference in Spring Valley, 1993. Without the request and encouragement of the colleagues on the Council, I might never have embarked on the attempt to put this theme in writing.

My special indebtedness goes to MaryJo Rogers of Sacramento for her editing of the original text. Further, valuable editorial assistance was contributed by Nancy Sommers of Washington, DC. Without the help of both these former students of Rudolf Steiner College, the task which I set myself could not have been completed. In addition, as they are both familiar with this theme, they made valuable suggestions which I was glad to incorporate. My special thanks go to both of them. A final word of gratitude—last but not least—to Sydney Mark for her devoted and tireless efforts in typing and preparing the manuscript.

R. M. Querido
Boulder, Colorado
Midsummer, 1995

Contents

Preface

On the occasion of the Annual Teachers' Conference in the summer of 1993, I was asked to give a series of five lectures on the theme: "What is the significance of a Christ-centered impulse in Waldorf education?" The first lecture was addressed to members of the Pedagogical Section of the School of Spiritual Science and dealt with the question of how one might recognize one's relationship to the historical event of the Mystery of Golgotha. The next four lectures were given to some 350 practicing Waldorf teachers. They included a midsummer address, given on the eve of the Festival of St. John. The present seven-chapter book includes what was then given with the exception of the festival address. It has also been considerably enlarged in scope and the material has been totally recast with a view to providing renewed consideration of what is one of the most important themes in our education.

Rudolf Steiner dealt with the Christ Impulse in pedagogy even before the founding of the first Waldorf school in 1919. During the subsequent five years, however, he addressed the topic repeatedly. Yet, because he did not speak about this subject in a long, systematic statement, its essential presence can be overlooked. In his pedagogical lectures what Rudolf Steiner did was to draw our attention to the Christ Impulse, often in the form of a brief statement or meditation meant to enhance the awareness of the early teachers. And what was said then is at least as valid today, seventy-five years later.

I have made an attempt to bring many of these indications together and especially to follow the "golden thread" of teaching out of the background of the Father (and Mother) forces in the early grades, of the Son forces in the middle grades, and through the Holy Spirit in the high school. Three chapters have been devoted to the curriculum and the development of the child and teenager at these different stages.

Much of the book is the result of experiences gathered during the last forty-five years. My special gratitude goes to some of the earliest teachers, whom I had the privilege of meeting and who were always prepared to answer the many questions of an eager beginner: W. J. Stein, Herbert Hahn, Ernst Lehrs, and Maria Lehrs. I would also like to acknowledge with deep thankfulness my colleagues of many years at Michael Hall, England. I owe a special debt of gratitude to having worked with A. W. Mann, L. F. Edmunds, and to Jesse Darrell for the many conversations on the ethical-religious impulses in the education. To a young teacher it was a tremendous inspiration to have lived in the presence of these friends, models indeed of the striving that imbues the very essence of our work with the children.

I have decided in this book not to deal with two facets of our work: the celebration of the festivals and the role of the independent religious education and services as given by Rudolf Steiner. It is clear that there is a need for both themes to be discussed in depth at the level of the College of Teachers. We cannot, out of habit or tradition, continue year in and year out to celebrate festivals unless we understand their profound significance and are able to convey their importance to the parents.

Equally, at a time when on the part of some parents there is a longing to find a re-emergence of ethical and religious values in education, the theme of the independent religion lessons and services should be broached. But there again it requires clarity and unanimity on the part of the College of Teachers first.

Nevertheless, it is hoped that the present book might contribute to forming a basis for some of these considerations. Obviously there can be no claim to being comprehensive in what I have said. I hope, rather, that the present work will provoke conversation, discussion, and further study, so that at this crucial time when we are entering the next millennium, our pedagogical movement may gain renewed insights and put them into practice for the healing and harmonizing of future generations, out of the active working of the spirit.

The leitmotif of this book is inspired from passages in the fifth lecture of *Education as a Social Problem,* given by Rudolf Steiner in Dornach on 16 August, 1919, shortly before the opening of the first Waldorf school in Stuttgart:

> One should not look superficially at the so-called cultural phenomena of our age. Nor should one doubt that modern human beings have to arouse themselves to a real comprehension of the Christ Impulse if evolution is to go forward in a healthy way. . . .
>
> This is also something future educators and teachers must take into their consciousness. . . . One must teach out of an awareness that one has to

bring about salvation in the case of every individual child; one has to steer him towards finding the Christ Impulse in the course of his life, towards finding a re-birth within himself. . . .

Such things must not live in the teacher as mere theory; they can be introduced into one's teaching only if one is strongly taken hold of by them in one's own soul. . . .'The best in me as a human being of this and following incarnations is what I find in myself as the Christ Impulse.'. . .We must, however, be clear that this Christ Impulse must not be the dogmatism of some religious body. . . .

Human intelligence left to itself travels on the path towards the Ahrimanic; it can become active for the good only through taking in the true Christ Impulse.

R. M. Querido
Boulder, Colorado
Midsummer, 1995

Introduction

Prelude — Some Fundamental Considerations

The Being of Christ, the Christ Impulse, and the Mystery of Golgotha are vast subjects that Rudolf Steiner deals with in varied ways in books and lectures from 1900 until his death in 1925. Before proceeding with the central theme of this book, it is important for us to ask what Rudolf Steiner means when he speaks of these profound, far-reaching topics. In the brief review which follows we begin to understand Steiner's Christology in an esoteric, historical context, and we become aware of Steiner's evolving development of these themes in his writings. Moreover, there emerges the awareness that, even when Steiner does not mention the Christ, he speaks and works directly out of the Christ Impulse in our time. From this remarkable concept we realize that our understanding of the Christ will gain new depths when we work appropriately within any aspect of the wide diversity which Steiner has brought to mankind.

Kali Yuga, an age of increasing spiritual darkness lasting five thousand years, ended in 1899 A.D., the year marking the dawning of the Light Age. One year later, Rudolf Steiner published a book entitled *Christianity as Mystical Fact*, a summation of lectures he had given in Berlin. The book, fundamental to understanding Steiner's views of Christianity, was inspired in part by Steiner's own experience of the Christ.

Though Steiner had been raised in the Catholic

tradition, in his youth he turned away from any formal religious institution. It was only when he reached the age of thirty-seven or thirty-eight that he made a renewed connection with the Christ Impulse out of a profound inner experience. Rudolf Steiner mentions this experience in his *Autobiography*:

> During the period when my statements about Christianity seemingly contradict my later ones, a conscious knowledge of true Christianity began to dawn within me. Around the turn of the century this knowledge grew deeper. The inner test described above occurred shortly before the turn of the century. This experience culminated in my standing in the spiritual presence of the Mystery of Golgotha in a most profound and solemn festival of knowledge.

The first few chapters of *Christianity as Mystical Fact* deal with the wisdom of the pre-Christian mysteries, such as the Greek sagas before Plato, then with Plato as a mystic, and then with Egyptian mystery wisdom. In the later chapters on the Gospels and particularly with the miracle of the raising of Lazarus, Rudolf Steiner shows clearly that the Christ event arises out of the ancient mysteries and creates a turning point for the whole evolution of mankind.

He distinguishes clearly between Christ, a cosmic being, and Jesus of Nazareth, the son of a carpenter. Jesus was a man of very considerable spiritual development who lived on earth for thirty years as a rabbi. He led an itinerant life until in the river Jordan, having been baptized by John, he received into his earthly being the fullness of the Christ, who lived within him for a period of three years. Even these brief statements show that Steiner's Christology is very different from the views held by most Christian denominations. Rudolf Steiner discourses further and at great length on the nature of the Christ Being, especially between the years 1907 and 1914, in a series of lecture courses he gives on the Gospels, starting with St. John and the Apocalypse and continuing through the Luke, Matthew, and Mark Gospels. In addition, Steiner gives a most important cycle of eleven lectures entitled *From Jesus to Christ*, and a series entitled *The Reappearance of Christ in the Etheric*. These many lecture cycles culminate in lectures given in 1913 and 1914 on what Steiner calls the "Fifth Gospel."

It is important to realize that Rudolf Steiner's research is not simply based on available texts, but on his own spiritual investigation, which he develops by dint of strenuous inner discipline as outlined, for instance, in his book, *Knowledge of Higher Worlds and Its Attainment*. Yet, again and again he shows that his spiritual research can be corroborated by the Gospels and other texts and that anyone with sound common sense can understand the new aspects he brings forth so plentifully.

Often Steiner speaks of what he calls "the Mystery of Golgotha." He characterizes it as the turning point in humanity's evolution, the most important event ever to occur for the world. The Mystery of Golgotha comprises the events in the life of Christ including His death and resurrection on the hill of Golgotha (which in Hebrew means "the place of the skull") in the heart of Jerusalem.

If we look more closely at the moment of the death on

Golgotha, particularly as described in the John Gospel and a number of apocryphal writings, we learn that the blood that flowed from the wounds of Christ Jesus at the crucifixion on Good Friday was in part collected in a chalice of great price by Joseph of Arimathea. This chalice, known as the Grail, was carried by Joseph on his travels toward the west. Eventually arriving at Glastonbury, Joseph founded the first Grail community in service of the purified blood of Christ. Since then, untold legends and sagas have arisen about the Grail and hidden Christian groups connected with it. Altogether, they point to the stream of esoteric Christianity which can be traced through the centuries, though not always in a continuous thread, even into the nineteenth century.

Highlights of this stream are represented by the works of Wolfram von Eschenbach, Chrétien de Troyes, Sir Thomas Malory, and later, the poetic works of Tennyson and the great music drama *Parsifal* by Richard Wagner.

Such works and many others record the workings of the Christ Impulse. In other words, the living Being of the Christ by no means ceases to affect what happens on Earth after His resurrection, but continues to work powerfully through the ages. This is what is called "the Christ Impulse." It can be seen especially in the hearts and minds of human beings. We can develop eyes that recognize this impulse as it works in the world.

It would go beyond the framework of our theme to consider the historical relevance of Christianity from its beginnings to our own time. Suffice it to say that much understanding has been lost of the true Christ Impulse through the ages, and much that is done "in His name," such as in the many religious quarrels that have arisen in

Christianity itself, cannot be attributed to the working of the Resurrected One, but arise out of the weakness and fanaticism of human beings.

Awareness of the Christ Impulse has been kept alive in a number of circles within esoteric Christianity, however. We could instance as the carriers of this impulse the religious leader Mani, initiates of the Grail stream, the Chartres Masters, Thomas Aquinas, the Templars, the genuine Rosicrucians, and students and teachers in the Platonic Academy in Florence during the Italian Renaissance.

Let us return for a moment to the cross on Golgotha. If we look closely again in our imaginations, we see that, while some of the blood of Christ was caught up in the Grail by Joseph, another portion flowed into the earth itself. Just as His body found its grave, so did His blood; both went into the very substance of the earth. This points to one of the greatest mysteries: the Christ Being united Himself with the earth, providing a kind of leaven for its transformation and renewal. In conjunction, His deed makes it possible for the soul of every human being to partake of His healing and atoning Impulse. Steiner makes it clear repeatedly that the Christ came for all people, irrespective of whether the individual is conscious of it or not. Nevertheless, it is the task of each single individual to awaken to this reality and create a living, inner awareness of the connection.

This insight may help us understand why Steiner refers to the Mystery of Golgotha as both "mystical" and "fact." It is mystical in as much as its effects embrace the totality of the supersensible world, the hierarchies, the unborn, and those who have died. It is a "fact" in as much as it took place like a great drama on the earthly, physical stage. To reconcile these two aspects is one of the most difficult of all quests, but now in the age of the consciousness soul, we should begin to undertake their reunion.

It may seem surprising to many, but Rudolf Steiner also embarked upon a Fifth Gospel. He gave indications regarding his work with it in a most tentative manner, filled with humility, pointing out that, although the four Gospels contain tremendous mysteries, a beginning should be made with a gospel appropriate to our day and age. This gospel, he says, will be fully written only in the future. Revelations such as this may be said to constitute a further aspect of the ongoing Christ Impulse.

Heraclitus, the great Greek philosopher, maintained that "everything is in flux;" everything is constantly changing, constantly evolving. Through Rudolf Steiner's works, one realizes that, just as this flux applies to nature, to the starry realms and our own lives on earth, it is also true of the hierarchies, even of the Christ Himself. It may be difficult to imagine at first, but the Christ is not the same as He was during the Mystery of Golgotha. He Himself has also evolved. Consequently, for those who have a living relationship with Him, understanding is ever born anew: "And behold, I make all things new." The reappearance of the Christ in the etheric as the Healer and Comforter has been possible in an ever-increasing way since the beginning of this century, the dawn of the Light Age.

The Waldorf teacher needs to be aware that Christology is at the heart of Anthroposophy. Its truths help form a healthy inner life.

Chapter I

A Meditative Approach

The relationship people establish with Anthroposophy varies greatly from one individual to another. For some, on meeting the work of Rudolf Steiner, the connection is immediate. One feels: I have always known this; it strikes a chord in my being. The experience may be compared to that of memory; one has known it, though before reading Steiner's work, one was unable to articulate it clearly. This awareness can be the beginning of a path of further study and inquiry. When doubts occur along this way, the question arises: How can I strengthen what I have apprehended so clearly at the outset?

On the other side of the scale, we have those who find it exceedingly difficult to make a connection. How is it possible for Rudolf Steiner to know all these things and express them with such conviction? Has he made errors in one field or another? Am I supposed to believe all this?

As Waldorf teachers we should remind ourselves again and again that we are only at the beginning. When this educational movement was founded in 1919, only twenty years had elapsed since the beginning of the Light Age which marked a dramatic turn in the affairs of mankind. We are all pioneers, and sooner or later one realizes that the goals for a wholesome, balanced education of children and youngsters, which Rudolf Steiner outlined in so many different ways, can be only partly realized. His indications are seeds for the future and will have to be tended anew by each generation. Our quest is not without struggle, and the trials come in a variety of ways.

One should perhaps ask: What is the difference between a Waldorf teacher and one who works in the pedagogical world at large? Is it a matter of curriculum? Of method? Of approach to the growing child? These are certainly factors that show a distinction. Yet, perhaps most essential is that the Waldorf teacher discovers his or her own profound need to embark upon a meditative path.

Practices in meditation today are remarkably varied. Some follow ancient traditions, failing to acknowledge the modern consciousness of our own day and age. For the Waldorf teacher actively working out of Anthroposophy, it cannot be a question of seeking stages of "blessedness" leading to a Nirvana away from this world. It also cannot be a question of inducing various stages of clairvoyance through taking substances that enhance consciousness artificially. Rudolf Steiner presents us with a middle path between Lucifer and Ahriman that can be trodden by anyone with sound common sense. It relates equally to the mysteries of the earth and to those of the spiritual world. It is in fact a Christ-centered path that establishes an equilibrium between these two opposing forces. One soon discovers that the equilibrium cannot be established once and for all. Nothing along this way is static. Efforts need to be renewed again and again. We are here dealing with a dynamic equilibrium.

By way of example let me quote a verse given by Rudolf Steiner:

> In the beginning was Christ,
> And Christ was with the Gods,
> And a God was Christ.

Deep in each human soul
The Being of Christ indwells.
In my soul too He dwells
And He will lead me
To the true meaning of my life.

These nine lines are endowed with great power. One notices how opening with the "beginning" (as in the John Gospel, "In the beginning was the Word,") we are led stage by stage downward, guided by the Christ, Who lives in every human soul. From there a further step is taken, a more intimate, inward one which points to the fact that the Christ lives also in me and can become the guide in my destiny. These lines are not meant to be analyzed intellectually. They are intended to be planted as seeds in the soul. Repeated contemplation upon them can reveal something growing in us. It can lead to an experience of inner certainty. Again, it is not a question of belief but of experience.

Such discussion is, of course, only a sketchy indication. Without an attitude of wonder, devotion, and patience, a meditative path will hardly be fruitful. We should perhaps emphasize the importance of regular, daily practice. One of the first indications that Rudolf Steiner gave as a condition for spiritual development is:

Rhythm replaces strength.

This regular tending and fostering of seeds in the soul may be compared to the activities of gardening. Within the inner realm also one makes sure that the ground is in good condition; removes the weeds, the roots, and rocks; supplies enough water; and exposes the process to the sun for a healthy growth to ensue. This preparatory activity is done by the six basic exercises:

1. Controlling thought
2. Focusing the will
3. Developing equanimity in the feeling life
4. Developing a positive, tolerant attitude
5. Becoming unbiased and ridding oneself of prejudice
6. Harmonizing the above five exercises so that they develop into an attitude of mind.

Details relating to these all-important preparatory exercises can be found in *Knowledge of Higher Worlds and Its Attainment* and in *Occult Science*. The six basic exercises lead to the development of the twelve-petaled lotus flower. This has been called the Christ chakra, located in the region of the heart.

A little reflection shows how important these attitudes of soul can be for the life of the Waldorf teacher. They directly influence our work with the children in the classroom and our relationships with one another as colleagues.

When all is said and done, studying Anthroposophy in its many forms is not a matter of acquiring beliefs, but much rather of asking: How can I experience the realities of the supersensible world? It is helpful in the quest to take the many indications offered by Rudolf Steiner in the spirit of "working hypotheses." In other words, we say to ourselves: I am going to try it and see what it leads to, not simply for my own enhancement, but so that I may become more effective, more insightful, and more compassionate in the calling I have chosen.

Striving and Grace on the Inner Path

In Wolfram von Eschenbach's *Parzival* we are shown how a young man, a fool at heart, sets out on a quest. Following his initial adventures, he turns to a search for his mother, not knowing that she has already died. His consciousness is clouded by a kind of dullness, and he even is confused about his true search. Finally, after much wandering, he meets Trevrizent, the Grail teacher, with whom he stays for two weeks because he has become mature enough to receive profound instruction.

He gains glimpses into the past, present, and future not only of his own life but also of the development of human history. He becomes aware that his quest is to find the Holy Chalice, the blood of Christ, the healing and restoring balm. Paradoxically, he is told by Trevrizent that one cannot strive for the Grail. What is meant?

On a genuine spiritual path that is Christ-centered, one cannot at any time force the process of spiritual development or enlightenment. We need to make every reasonable effort without straining the inner process. Whether results are obtained or not depends entirely on grace, on whether or not the spiritual world bestows, in accordance with one's karma, a certain revelation. This is a path calling for much humility and patience.

This spiritual principle of non-coercion, if we reflect upon it, is of the greatest importance for the teacher. Suppose a certain problem arises with a child. We are at a loss as to what to do. We meditate every evening upon the circumstances at hand, but we cannot force a solution. It may take weeks or months before—perhaps quite suddenly as a result of our inner work—one day the riddle begins to

5

be solved. We know for certain what to do. We might describe it that the angel of the child was able in our night consciousness to convey a message to us which we were able to receive upon waking in the morning. Remembering it, we could then act upon it.

The Workings of the Christ Impulse

The Christ inspiration can be seen very clearly in certain works of art, music, and literature. As examples, one could turn to the paintings of Raphael, Leonardo da Vinci, Dürer, Grünewald, and many others. In music we may easily recognize that J. S. Bach, Mozart, and Bruckner were Christ-inspired. Yet we need to widen our perspective.

Shortly before his death in 1961, Dr. F. W. Zeylmans van Emmichoven, a close pupil of Rudolf Steiner, completed a book whose English title reads, *The Reality in Which We Live*. This work contained the fruit of Dr. Zeylmans' long career as a physician and psychiatrist. Appointed by Rudolf Steiner as the General Secretary of the Dutch Society in 1923, when he was in his late twenties, he rose to become a leading anthroposophist with an international reputation.

In a personal word of introduction, the book opens as follows:

> At a certain stage of my development I came to the inner realization that Christ is the reality in which we live. As I write this sentence, I am aware that it will hardly be possible to express all I mean by it.

It far outreaches the context of this study to summarize the contents of Dr. Zeylmans' remarkable book, but it might be helpful to touch upon one or two examples.

Was Goethe (1749-1832) a Christian or not? Scholars have argued the matter one way or another for over a hundred years. He was no churchgoer, though he read the Bible on an almost daily basis. His poems and other writings do not speak directly of Christ Jesus. However, much is in them, if we have eyes to see. Faust, for example, though intent on committing suicide, pulls back when he hears the bells ring out early on Easter morning.

Among the many discoveries that Goethe made, one has a special place in his rich and varied biography. After his Italian journey, which changed his life, he wrote *The Metamorphosis of the Plants* both in prose and poetic forms. The book arose from his profound experience at the Botanical Gardens of Palermo, Sicily, where he discovered the archetypal plant. It may seem surprising to characterize this discovery as Christ-inspired. Yet upon reflection we might recognize that the Christ Impulse works essentially through time, through transformation, and through evolution, and that what is true in the life structure of plants also appears in the life cycles through which people pass in the course of their incarnations.

Another example of the presence of the Christ Impulse can be found in the works of William Shakespeare, born on 23 April (St. George's Day), 1564. Interestingly enough, he also died in his native Stratford-on-Avon on St. George's Day, 1616. In his plays we find hardly any mention of the Christ, and the word "Christian" appears only once or twice. But was Shakespeare a Christian? This question has also been hotly debated. At his own wish he was buried in Trinity Church, Stratford, but it does not appear that he was a traditional, church-attending Christian.

If we turn to Shakespeare's plays, however, we can detect the Christ Impulse. His plays contain themes of transformation and renewal. The mysteries of love, sacrifice, and forgiveness in their many forms are central as well.

Romeo and Juliet, from one viewpoint, sacrificed their own lives so that the bitter and fatal feud between their families might be healed. *Othello*, a meditation on the green-eyed monster of jealousy, brings the leading characters to death as the outcome of a karmic fault that can only find compensation in a future life. We see the catastrophe resulting from the absence of love.

In *King Lear*, the theme of blindness of body and soul informs the play. Lear is blind to the genuine love Cordelia bears him and falls for the wiles of his two evil daughters. It is only after the most harrowing trials that King Lear recognizes the true and noble nature of Cordelia.

In characters such as Cordelia, Portia, and Hermione, the deepest aspects of Christian love and sacrifice find expression. Similarly, in *The Tempest* Prospero has the nobility of heart to forgive those who had intended to kill him.

Continuing our musings by turning to the world of art, would we say that the work of Vincent van Gogh (1853–1890) reveals a Christian impulse? It could well be argued that he painted the theme of Christ in only a couple of paintings, one a rendition of a work by Delacroix. What of his many landscapes, portraits, and self-portraits which he painted in Paris and later in Provence?

Over time it has become clear that van Gogh has made a unique contribution to humanity. His paintings are sun-imbued to such an extent that the beholder who has an open mind and heart is led to see nature in a new way. It is as if van Gogh was able to depict the workings of the Christ Impulse in the weavings of nature itself. His works, in spite of his tragic biography, are endowed with a profoundly pure feeling element. In his portraits, one could say that he is seeking to reveal the essential "I am" of the sitter. In his self-portraits, this quest may be seen as his attempt to express the essential, immortal nature of his own being through the outer façade of his earthly personality.

Many other examples could be cited, but for the moment it may be sufficient to have attempted to look, perhaps in a new way, at the works of Goethe, Shakespeare, and van Gogh as Christ-permeated individualities.

In conclusion, it is helpful, as we look for the Christ Impulse weaving through history, if—in addition to developing an awareness of the Christ Being in history— we become aware of His ever-abiding presence and life-sustaining effect in our own lives. This awareness can occur in any moment, but it often comes when we are able to still the soul so that it may receive the reality of the Christ. Let me end by quoting one of the most moving passages by Rudolf Steiner about the Christ:

> Christ knows us. To a soul that sees our Spiritual Science in the true light, to a heart that feels it in its true significance, I can impart no more esoteric saying:
> "The Christ is seeing us."

Chapter II

Our Modern Consciousness

One of the most important discoveries we can make by means of Spiritual Science is that in the course of its development humanity has gone through different stages of consciousness. This is not only true regarding the longer spans of history, such as the ancient Egyptian and Greco-Latin periods, but also for shorter periods.

Since 1413 A.D., humanity has lived in the period of the birth of the consciousness soul. It dawned gradually during the Renaissance and bore the scientific age. Since its inception, humanity has become more and more conscious of the physical, material world that surrounds us. We have grown more and more aware of our own individuality.

In 1879 A.D. we entered the Age of Michael which lasts approximately as many years as there are days in the year. As a Sun Being, the Time Spirit Michael is not interested in family traditions, in conventions, in race, or nation, but solely in the gifts of the individual who strives towards the spirit while remaining firmly planted on the physical plane.

The paradoxes are not easy to reconcile. The consciousness soul (which can also be termed the spiritual soul) can only be developed by the individual. It cannot be given from outside or through the bloodline. Although it is the highest of the soul forces, which ultimately will lead to a uniting with the spirit, it can only be acquired by standing

11

firmly on the physical plane and learning to face evil.

This situation creates many anxieties and tensions for the modern soul. The first steps can be harrowing and bring about alienation from one's fellow human beings, from nature, and also from one's inner self. It is telling that in the first third of this century existentialism was born and that Jean Paul Sartre wrote such works as *No Exit* and *Nausea*. Pablo Picasso was perhaps the first painter to portray men and women with distorted faces, depicting the agonizing split of the personality.

Rudolf Steiner remarked that humanity is "crossing the threshold" and that this condition began to take place during the middle of the last century, around 1848. What does this really mean? Collectively, humanity is becoming more aware of the forces of good and evil that cast their shadow into our everyday lives. The many wars that have been waged at accelerating, recurring intervals since the beginning of this century point dramatically to this tragic phenomenon.

Since the fearful two world wars that shook the globe, dozens of conflicts in different parts of the world have erupted, bringing suffering and tragedy to millions. These have been brought about by a withdrawal of the benevolent guiding powers and an increased activity of the Ahrimanic forces that seek to enslave humanity. These conflicts show clearly that we have to overcome our racial, national, ethnic prejudices in order to find what is truly human in each one of us.

But also the individual soul finds an ever greater tension arising in his own being. Many people at an early age become aware that two souls live within each of us;

one that aspires to the loftiest heights of humanity, while the other seeks to fetter us ever more strongly to material existence. The crossing of the threshold is experienced to begin with as a split in our normal consciousness. We need to learn not only to face the evil in others but also in ourselves. This struggle needs to be taken up with courage and determination. To imagine that it can be circumvented or overlooked is simply an illusion.

This places the task of the Waldorf teacher in a new light. Each one of us is centrally involved in the Michaelic battle against the forces of darkness for the sake of the children and youngsters in our care.

In that connection our inner work plays a crucial role. Much help can be found in the many verses and meditations given by Rudolf Steiner. They can be applied to different situations. In the field of pedagogy, we find those that apply particularly to the individual teacher, others for establishing a fruitful relationship between colleagues, and yet others that serve for enhancing and quickening our relationship to the children in our care.

The following meditation, which is one of the last ones given by Rudolf Steiner (in Stuttgart on 11 April, 1924 and in Bern on 17 April, 1924), sums up in a most concise way the path that needs to be followed in order to bring healing to the social sickness of our time.

DARKNESS, LIGHT, LOVE

To bind oneself to matter
Means to grind the soul to dust.

To find oneself in the spirit
Means to unite human beings.

To behold oneself in man
Means to build worlds.

These six lines express the challenge to every human being today who aspires towards the development of the consciousness soul which, when acquired, brings enlightenment and love into the world.

Our Relationship to the Hierarchies

In a play that was produced in Oxford and London shortly after the Second World War, Christopher Fry in *A Sleep of Prisoners* was able to express in one of Meadows' speeches the essence of our modern crisis.

> The human heart can go to the lengths of God.
> Dark and cold we may be, but this
> Is no winter now. The frozen misery
> Of centuries breaks, cracks, begins to move;
> The thunder is the thunder of the floes,
> The Thaw, the flood, the upstart Spring.
> Thank God our time is now when wrong
> Comes up to face us everywhere,
> Never to leave us till we take
> The longest stride of soul men ever took.
> Affairs are now soul size.
> The enterprise
> Is exploration into God.
> Where are you making for? It takes
> So many thousand years to wake,
> But will you wake for pity's sake?
> Wake up, will you? . . .
> Where do you think you're going?

This powerful speech could be felt in the post-war years as a newly kindled torch igniting the enthusiasm of a younger generation. It is interesting to reflect that most Waldorf teachers practicing on the North American continent now were born round about the time when this play first appeared. When Steiner was asked when the end of the century would really begin, he pointed to 1950 as a dramatic turning point.

The speech quoted above is full of powerful imaginations. What can be meant by "the enterprise is exploration unto God?" This has special significance for the Waldorf teacher who needs, with courage of heart, to take this leap.

Steiner characterized it immediately upon inaugurating the first Waldorf school in Stuttgart in 1919. He called upon the founding circle of twelve teachers always to remember that their karma had placed them in that situation and that they would have to reckon with the reality of the spiritual world. He advised them that in the evening, before proceeding with the meditation they had chosen, they should beseech Angels, Archangels, and Archai to help them in their activities for the following day; and that in the morning, after their meditation, they would know themselves to be connected with the Beings of the Third Hierarchy.

This theme was developed a week later in members lectures given in Berlin between 12 and 14 September, 1919. The relationship that has to be established with the Hierarchies is one of the most important aspects of our inner work. It has a number of different facets. We should reflect again and again upon the fact that, before their incarnation, souls on their descent to earth commune with the Beings of the Third Hierarchy. These Beings carry the

15

souls of children into earthly life, having endowed them in accordance with their karma with gifts and talents, with possibilities and predilections.

The words of William Wordsworth's *Ode* are not simply a beautiful poetic image:

> Our birth is but a sleep and a forgetting:
> The Soul that rises with us, our life's Star,
>   Hath had elsewhere its setting,
>   And cometh from afar:
>   Not in entire forgetfulness,
>   And not in utter nakedness,
> But trailing clouds of glory do we come
>   From God, who is our home:
> Heaven lies about us in our infancy!

They do indeed reflect a profound spiritual reality. One aspect of Waldorf education consists of continuing the work of the Hierarchies (as Steiner put it), but in attempting such an awesome task, we have to explore the nature of the Hierarchies, their function in the cosmos and in human life. How can their influences become palpable? The Angels weave in our thinking, Archangels participate in our feeling life, and the Archai take part in our deeds and moral impulses.

Their activity is reflected in an archetypal way during the first three years of the child. The Archai provide us with our uprightness in walking in the first year. The development of speech in the second year is bestowed on us by the Archangels, and the individual thinking activity, which is born in the third year, can be attributed to the working and weaving of the Angels.

Repeatedly, Steiner has pointed out that these first three

years are of immense importance in the subsequent life of the individual. More is learned at this time than at any other. In fact, life as it unfolds through the various periods is nothing but a constant set of variations on the themes of walking and movement, of speech and feeling, and of thinking and reflection.

But we should remind ourselves that the ninefold hierarchical choirs, divided into three Hierarchies, are members of God, members of the Cosmic Christ Himself. Indeed, the Christ accompanies, through the working of Archai, Archangels, and Angels, the first three years of the child in a special, intimate manner. Here the basis is laid for the three great I Am words:

I am the Way. I am the Truth. I am the Life.

Furthermore, in the communion-forming imagination that Rudolf Steiner gave to the founding teachers, we find a sublime image of the inter-weaving of the Third Hierarchy: the Angels bestowing strength, the Archangels courage, and the Archai light. (A detailed account can be found in *Towards the Deepening of Waldorf Education*, based on the recollection of those who were present at this profound ceremony.)

The "exploration into God" for Waldorf teachers is to familiarize ourselves more and more with "unborn-ness," a supersensible phase through which souls travel before incarnation.

It may be appropriate to conclude this section by quoting two aphorisms by Rudolf Steiner:

To meditate means to warm the thought in one's heart.

17

And:

> Knowledge (recognition) is the light and love the
> warmth of that light.

Where and When Is the Christ Impulse Mentioned?

From our earlier considerations it will have become evident that the healing, compassionate, and loving Impulse of the Christ is mentioned to the teachers by Rudolf Steiner on very few occasions. It is only during the last three years of Steiner's activity that he speaks clearly of its importance. At Easter of 1923, Steiner gave a series of eight lectures to a large public audience of teachers in Switzerland, published under the title *The Child's Changing Consciousness and Waldorf Education*.

In the sixth lecture, given on 20 April, 1923, we find a rather surprising indication. On this occasion, he gave a prayer or meditation for all teachers. It was not restricted only to those working in the Waldorf movement and goes as follows:

> **Dear Lord may I, with regard to my personal ambitions, completely extinguish myself. And may the Christ make true in me the words of St. Paul: "Not I, but Christ in me."** (This prayer is addressed to God in general and to the Christ in particular.) **So that the Holy Spirit may hold sway in the teacher. This is the true threefoldness.**

This meditation or prayer opens the path for relating to the divine Father or Mother ground of worlds, to the Cosmic Christ, and to the grace of the Holy Spirit, the Sophia, in the practice of educating children. We beseech the forces of the Trinity to help us in our task.

It may be helpful to consider this prayer or meditation a

little further. What is really meant by extinguishing one's personal ambitions? Having pondered this, it occurs to me that it is of special significance in working with our colleagues. In a school where the social relationships are harmonious it cannot be a question of teachers vying with one another. For instance, to aim at being the best teacher, the most popular one with the students, to aspire to become the chairman of the faculty or college, to gain a position— all this, all such striving, should be eradicated. It is far more important for colleagues in their working together to recognize the individual's gifts and aptitudes so that we might take up a particular responsibility. It should never be a question of power politics, but to ask ourselves how can we best serve.

The passage "May the Christ make true in me," and the words of St. Paul: "Not I, but Christ in me," seem to be a call gradually to overcome the "little self," so that the "higher self" might become operative. It is the key to self-development. The road may indeed be a long one, beset by many trials, but we should attempt it and embark upon it, although we recognize that the ultimate ideal may be difficult to realize completely. Here the Christ is a constant help.

The passage with regard to the Holy Spirit points, perhaps in a special way, to the "imponderables" of the education. We most probably have all experienced moments in the classroom which are special, unique, and cannot possibly be reproduced. There are those blessed moments arising out of a particular situation where students and teacher are at one; a type of communion seems to arise. We should remember that the working of the Holy Spirit is always new and unexpected—a moment of grace which is nevertheless clearly perceived when it occurs.

In the eighth lecture, given on 22 April, 1923, we find stimulating indications on how to work actively with the Gospels in relation to particular situations that occur in the classroom. These remarks are prefaced by the following passage which I think bears reflection:

> In this sense, the College of Teachers must become the spirit and soul of the entire school organism. Only then will each teacher enter the classroom with the right attitude and in the right soul condition. At the same time we must also bear in mind that just in these matters an intensely religious element can be found. There is no need to have the name of the Lord constantly upon one's lips nor of calling upon the name of Christ all the time. Better to adhere to the command: "Thou shalt not take the name of the Lord God in vain." Nevertheless, it is possible to permeate one's entire life with a fundamental religious impulse, with a most intensely Christian impulse.

In a very sketchy way, Rudolf Steiner gives indications of how we can find the right stimulation for finding appropriate forms of pedagogy in therapeutic areas, namely by allowing ourselves to be inspired time and again by what radiates from the Gospel of St. Luke.

In order to help students to develop the necessary idealism for life, we should turn again and again to the Gospel of St. John as a source of inspiration.

If we do not want our students to grow up into cowards but the kind of people who will tackle life's tasks with ebullient energy, we should turn towards the Gospel of St. Mark.

In order to help young people to grow into perceptive adults, rather than into people who go through life with unseeing eyes, we can receive the necessary stimulation from turning to the Gospel of St. Matthew.

Rudolf Steiner mentioned in this passage that to modern ears such statements might even sound grotesque, but let us consider more closely what fruit such indications provide.

It has often been remarked that there are "contradictions" in the stories reported by the different Evangelists. These outer difficulties disappear as soon as we begin to understand that each Evangelist, initiated in a particular aspect, viewed the mystery of the Christ Being from a different vantage point. In fact, each one was initiated in one of the four mysteries depicted by the Great Cross in terms of the zodiac.

The following diagram may be of assistance. St. Luke was able to work out of the transformed Bull influences that bring love and compassion. Mark gained his insight from the Lion forces of courage and strength, whereas Matthew, working out of the forces of Waterman, was able to describe the Being of Christ Jesus with great historical accuracy, showing how the many prophecies of the Old Testament came to fulfillment. John, the disciple who rested his head on the heart of Christ Jesus at the Last Supper, had been most deeply initiated and represents the transformation of Scorpio (that deals with death) into the Eagle of the resurrection who can survey the deepest mysteries.

LUKE	MARK
Compassion	Courage
(Bull)	(Lion)
Christ as Healer	Christ as Cosmic Power

THE COSMIC
SUN BEING

MATTHEW	JOHN
Observation,	Deepening,
Awareness	Reverence
(Waterman)	(Scorpio turned into Eagle)
Christ Jesus as Man	The Mystery of Christ

Let us now apply these indications to the work in the classroom. Supposing that in our third or fourth grade we find a major disturbance in the social fabric. Children treat one another unkindly, there is bullying going on, small gangs form against others. Naturally we have to deal with these matters pedagogically, but a further step could be taken. Because of the healing forces emanating from the Luke Gospel, we as teachers can meditate upon this Gospel. For instance, we read one chapter every night, recalling in the morning what has been read and continuing next evening with the next chapter and so on. In time we will find that our own meditative activity will bring an improvement in the social fabric of the class.

Equally, if we find that there is an increasing lack of

tidiness, the children do not see what is around them and they show a certain lack of care, working with the Matthew Gospel will improve the situation and it will gradually be noticed that the children become more observant, more aware.

If we notice that there is a certain lack of courage, students being unwilling to own up to some misdemeanor—for instance a window is broken and no one is prepared to stand up and say "I did it"—such situations can be helped by the teacher working for himself or herself, as part of the regular daily meditative preparation, on the Mark Gospel.

Imagine the situation of trying to tell a serious story where pain and suffering is involved, which can only be understood out of a sense of inner reverence, when suddenly the mood is changed by a student making a silly and totally inappropriate remark. It might be said in a mocking way and rouse a peal of laughter on the part of the other children. The lesson is spoiled. We can help to transform this lack of reverence and devotion by turning to the John Gospel, the most profound of all.

It must not be imagined that such means of "healing" will work quickly, for they act in a subtle manner and via sleep. As teachers, in the evening we concern ourselves with a particular Gospel content. We then go to sleep and meet the souls of the children who receive the healing thoughts that we have been pondering. Next morning, in clear consciousness, we see a change—however slight to begin with. If this is practiced regularly, much can be achieved.

Steiner's Final Address

At Easter time, 1923, Rudolf Steiner addressed the students, parents, and teachers for the last time. He spoke at the opening of the new school year, when the Stuttgart Waldorf School, in a period of five years, had grown to more than eight hundred students in twelve grades.

The concluding words are deeply moving and express the underlying ideals of the education.

> Students of the top grade, that means dear teachers. We wish to work courageously and with enthusiasm to imbue ourselves with the education—a preparation for the school of life.
>
> Thus may it be, for then the school will be led by the loftiest guide, by the Christ Himself.
>
> We wish to strive forwards, out of enthusiasm for the task in hand and also out of love for the children. . . .
>
> And so with love and enthusiasm in the hearts for the children, and with love and enthusiasm in the hearts of the teachers we shall continue to work together.

Chapter III

The Inner Structure of the Curriculum

We should bear in mind that in the lectures entitled *The Younger Generation*, October 1922, Rudolf Steiner explains that Waldorf education is not a method, but a striving to awaken children and teenagers. Because it is an awakening impulse, we should not force the curriculum into a rigid structural form in which everything must be done the same way by every teacher. In fact, the curriculum could be compared to a musical score which each master performer interprets differently. In its essence, it will be the same piece in each performance. The artistic freedom of each teacher lies in its interpretation.

If we consider an inner structure for the twelve grades, Steiner's indications for the syllabus of the religion lessons applies very well. From this point of view the first four grades form a totality, as do the fifth through eighth grades, and the four grades of the high school consist of a third group.

In the two verses that we say with the children at the beginning of the main lesson, both for the younger and older students, we find that in each the outer "sun-lit world" and the inner "soul realm" are addressed. The Being of God to Whom we appeal is mentioned in both. The morning verse for the younger children follows:

> The sun with loving light
> Makes bright for us each day;

The soul with spirit might
Gives strength unto my limbs.
In sunlight shining clear
I reverence, O God,
The strength of humankind
Which Thou so graciously
Has planted in my soul,
That I with all my might
May love to work and learn.
From Thee comes light and strength,
To Thee rise love and thanks.

Through this verse we see that the deeper aspects of the curriculum build a firm bridge for the students between the outer world perceived with the senses (the kingdoms of nature) and the inner world of soul and spirit. As teachers we must help the students learn to read two books. One is the Book of Nature which consists of minerals, plants, animals, mountains, and lakes in all their grand diversity throughout the world. The other, the Book of Civilization, includes history, literature, and the development of culture among different nations, races, religions, and languages. Broadly, the Book of Nature deals with Space, whereas the Book of Civilization deals more with Time. Nature and civilization are, of course, constantly interweaving, and much will depend on whether we are able in our lessons to allow them to relate in a flexible manner.

Summarizing, we might say that the Book of Nature deals with the sciences, such as botany, zoology, physiology, chemistry, and earth science, and can helpfully be referred to with the term "Geographia" (which means "earth writing"). By the Book of Civilization, we understand mythology, history, the history of the arts, and world literature, which can be encompassed by the term "Historia."

The Inner Structure of the First Four Grades

Book of Nature **GEOGRAPHIA**	Book of Civilization **HISTORIA**
Grade I	
Nature Stories	Fairy Stories Folk Tales
Grade II	
Nature Stories (Animals)	Fables Legends
Grade III	
House Building Farming The Cycle of the Year	The Old Testament
Grade IV	
Local History and Geography	Norse Mythology Man and Animal

The above table offers a few highlights of the curriculum as taught in the main lessons. Naturally, many other subjects could be added.

For our purpose, it may be sufficient to consider Steiner's indication that the material of the first four grades should be taught out of the inner background of the Father world, in other words, that all subjects arise out of the interplay of the creative forces of the Heavenly Father world and the Earth Mother.

In the first grade this is reflected very clearly in nature stories, fairy tales, and folk tales. In the second grade animal stories are not treated like zoology, but rather are meant to give the children a feeling for the habitat and life of animals. In the legends we are dealing with human beings who have shown particular abilities in rising above much of humanity by performing deeds of compassion, healing, and courage. We think of a St. Francis, a St. Elizabeth, and a St. Bridget. In every nation we find many examples of men and women who have served humanity in a special way. In the second grade it is not a question of the teacher's telling an extensive biographical story; that comes later.

The third grade illustrates clearly the aspect of the creative powers of the Godhead. The seven days of creation, magnificently told in the first book of Genesis, offer a grand inspiration for the stories that follow: Adam and Eve in Paradise, the expulsion from the Garden of Eden by the intervention of Lucifer (who opposes his will to the Godhead), the stories of Cain and Abel, of Noah and the Flood, of Abraham and his sons, and the finding of the Promised Land. At every turn in these remarkable events we can sense the guiding hand of God. In the dramatic story of Moses, we witness the remarkable release from Egyptian oppression. We travel through the Red Sea and hear of the joys and sufferings of a chosen people seeking, after wandering for forty years in the desert, a permanent abode. Without tracing the story further, it becomes evident that we are dealing with a very special schooling. The Hebrews had to learn to obey the voice and the presence of God. There is perhaps no story in the literature of the world that so clearly emphasizes the working of the Godhead through the elements.

If we now turn in the third grade curriculum to life on the farm, the rotation of crops, the caring for the animals, we find all of these activities embedded in the cycle of the year, in the great nature festivals of sowing and reaping, of the attitude and endeavors of the farmer and his family seeking to be in tune with the interplay of climate, weather, and earth. This can develop a sense of gratitude in us and the children, as we learn to rely on what the creative powers give us.

But before settling down and leaving our lives as nomads, we have to build a shelter for ourselves and our family. Only then can the cultivation of the earth around us begin. The building block that we teach in third grade encompasses the construction of many different houses and shelters in different parts of the world, not only in our own. We learn about igloos, houses on stilts, constructions in marble (in parts of Italy, where this building material is abundant), and wooden and brick houses. We also go into plans and building materials.

The above is mentioned to show that we are dealing with the world of nature and its transformation by the human hand. What was given by the creative forces of the Gods—stone, timber, the riches of the earth—is changed through the work of human beings the world over, men and women belonging to different races and creeds, speaking different languages, and living different lives from our own. All this helps the children become more tolerant of others and develop a sense of gratitude to all human beings.

In the fourth grade a further dimension is added. We now begin to explore our surroundings and the geography of the area in which we live. We learn to understand the contribution of native Americans and other peoples (such as the Chinese and the Russians, if our school is in California).

At this stage an important block is added that studies the relationship between the human and animal kingdoms, their differences and their interplay. We explore with the children all that the animal kingdom provides us. When we turn to the Norse stories in fourth grade, we hear of another creation myth, very different from Genesis. The gods and goddesses appear on the scene with their trials and fabulous experiences. Quite often a humorous note is added, as in the stories of Thor and Loki. But the dramatic saga ends with the twilight of the gods. The gods retreat and human beings must learn to stand on their own without the guidance of the divine powers enjoyed up to this point. This is just what a fourth grader may feel he or she is going through. Gradually, the Father world withdraws so that the human being might begin to play his central role.

The Creative Father and Mother Principle

We have seen that it would be preferable to teach the children from the first to the fourth grade (ages seven to ten, approximately) out of the mood of the Father forces, God living and weaving in nature. In a sense, pantheism is at home during these years. The forces of the Father God are woven through the subjects in the first four grades.

As a guideline, especially for the third grade when we deal with farming, the following verse by Rudolf Steiner, given at Christmas 1922, comes to mind. It was given on the occasion of the founding of a Waldorf school in England.

The plant roots quicken in the night of the earth,
The leaves unfold through the might of the air,
The fruits grow ripe through the power of the sun.

So quickens the soul in the shrine of the heart,
So man's spirit unfolds in the light of the world,
So ripens man's strength in the glory of God.

And root and leaf and the ripe fruit's blessing
Support the life of men on earth;
And soul and spirit and the strong deed's action
May raise themselves in gratitude to God.

In general, for these four grades, there is a guideline in the following words by Rudolf Steiner, from one of his notebooks, (Ilkley, England, 12 August, 1923).

The eye of man is glad
In the light cast by the shining sun.
So may our soul rejoice
In the spirit of God, who lives
In all, as sun unseen,
Casting its light in love for every being.

We should attend to the fact that children from the change of teeth to the tenth year pass through a very intensive stage psychologically—the nine-year change. This change usually brings with it the first glimmers of uncertainty: Are you really my daddy? Are you really my mommy? I think my teacher made a mistake this morning. The child needs to be reassured. I remember years ago that the son of one of my colleagues, on a beautiful summer's day in England, rushed in from the garden and said with a note of despair, "Mommy, the trees are no longer talking to me." It is interesting to note that this boy had never said that the trees had been speaking to him, but the loss of that communion was heartbreaking. It is not perhaps always expressed quite so clearly, but a loss of being in touch with nature can be profoundly felt at this age. In a rather remarkable way, the curriculum is able to ease this situation considerably. In the third grade, the Old Testament stories of the trials and tribulations of the Hebrew people give meaning to the soul's downward path into life on earth. Another note is sounded through the farming and the building blocks: Paradise has been lost and we need to enter life on earth through facing the challenges of work, suffering, and death.

While it is too early in third and fourth grade to introduce stories about Christ Jesus, the tales in *Christ Legends* by Selma Lagerlof could certainly be told, especially around Christmas. The four weeks of Advent with the Advent wreath and its four candles also offer a special opportunity to teach the children to sing some Christmas carols. It is at this darkest time of the year that Hanukkah, the festival of lights, can also be celebrated. Naturally, in introducing *The Shepherds Play*, one would also want to present the story of Mary, Joseph, and Jesus in the manger at Bethlehem.

"Wonders Are Many on Earth"

Steiner pointed out on many occasions that we should always place the human being in the center of our considerations in teaching children and youngsters. There is always this twofold relationship: the God-given world of

32

nature in her manifold aspects, and the activity of men and women on the earth. Perhaps none has expressed this so powerfully as Sophocles in one of the choruses of *Antigone*:

> Wonders are many on earth, and the greatest of these
> Is man, who rides the ocean and makes his way
> Through the deeps, through wind-swept valleys of
>   perilous
>   Seas that surge and sway.
> He is master of ageless Earth, to his own will bending
> The immortal mother of gods by the sweat of his brow,
> As year succeeds to year, with toil unending
>   Of mule and plough.
>
> He is lord of all things living; birds of the air,
> Beasts of the field, all creatures of sea and land
> He taketh, cunning to capture and ensnare
>   With the net of his mind.
> Hunting the savage beast from the upland rocks,
> Taming the mountain monarch in his lair,
> Teaching the wild horse and the roaming ox
>   His yoke to bear.
>
> The use of language, the wind-swift motion of thought
> There is nothing beyond his power. His subtlety
> Meeteth all chance, all danger conquereth.
>   For every ill he hath found its remedy,
>   Save only death.
> O wondrous intelligence of man, that draws
> To good or evil ways! Great honour is given
> And power to him who upholdeth his country's laws
>   And the justice of heaven.

Classroom Pictures from the First Four Grades

On 31 January, 1923, Rudolf Steiner gave a few suggestions regarding pictures on the walls appropriate to the different grades. For the first grade he suggested fairy tale pictures; for the second grade, pictures of legends; for the third grade, still lifes and plants; and for the fourth, paintings of animals. In addition, lighting a candle for special occasions is entirely appropriate. We should always strive to decorate the classroom in a pleasing, aesthetic manner. An indoor nature garden with moss and crystals, beautifully arranged, can certainly contribute to the mood of the room where we teach.

In our civilization, which pays so little attention to real values and quality, a special effort will have to be made in steering a secure course between triviality and sentimentality. Here an artistic feeling is the best guide.

Sacramentalism in Education

In the last lecture of a cycle entitled *The Karma of Vocation*, given on 27 November, 1916, Rudolf Steiner refers to sacramentalism in education in a rather special way. We note that this remark occurred three years before the opening of the first Waldorf school:

> It is already possible to make a beginning in many things. Most of all, human beings can begin to develop sacramentalism in two areas. The first is that of educating and teaching children. We will begin to spiritualize what the religions call "baptism" when we look upon every human being who enters the world through birth as bringing his or her Christ forces with him or herself. Thus we will have the right reverence before the growing

human being and can then direct the entire education and especially the teaching of the child in this spirit so that in the teaching we bring a sacramentalism to fruition. We can achieve the same end when we not only look upon educating and teaching the child as a divine service, but also *make* it such a divine service. Finally, when we endeavor to bring what we call our knowledge into our consciousness in such a way that, as our souls are filled with ideas of the spiritual world, we are aware that the spiritual world is entering into us and that we are being united with the spiritual; when we look upon that as a "communion". . . the symbolic sacrament of the altar will become the universal sacramental experience of knowledge. It is in this direction that the Christianizing of humanity must move forward. You will then come to the knowledge that everywhere in life, reality . . . enters in everything that is related to the Christ.

The above passage is far-reaching and points to the "imponderables" of the education. So much depends on our attitude, on our frame of mind, and though these attitudes or moods of soul are not directly expressed, they work deeply on the children in our care. If we as teachers can truly develop a feeling for what the child, through birth, is bringing with him or her through the Christ forces, a valuable undertone is created that will assist us in our task.

This passage will lead us over to the next chapter where we shall concern ourselves with the Christ Impulse as it permeates the curriculum of grades five to eight.

Although the theme of this book does not concern itself directly with the celebration of the festivals and the cultivation of the spiritual life, out of our attitude towards nature, imbued through and through with the forces of the divine, appropriate festivals can be arranged. A sense of wonder, reverence, and gratitude should permeate everything we do with the children. A universal approach is essential, without any denominational undertone.

Finally, it is worth considering the deeper meaning of what Steiner said in a public lecture in Dornach, given on the first of July, 1923, under the title of "Why Do We Need an Anthroposophical Pedagogy?" It offers a unique perspective. If approximately between the ages of seven and fourteen the child is not introduced in a living way to the Christ, along the lines of the Waldorf curriculum, in later life the youngster is more likely either to deny the Christ or to hold onto a traditional faith by means of which he or she cannot truly experience the Resurrected One. It may be worthwhile to reflect upon this in our faculty meetings.

Chapter IV

The Inner Structure of Grades Five to Eight

As the students enter the fifth grade, a new verse, which we say with the students, forms the beginning of each main lesson. Although it is still based on the outer and the inner worlds that the students are to discover, its character is quite different from that of the verse said in the first four grades. Instead of "The sun with loving light makes bright for me each day," used in the first four grades, we now turn to:

> I do behold the world
> wherein there shines the sun,
> wherein there gleam the stars,
> wherein there lie the stones.
> The plants they live and grow,
> The beasts they feel and live,
> And man to spirit gives
> A dwelling in his soul.
> I do behold the soul
> That dwelleth within me.
> God's spirit lives and weaves
> In heights of world without,
> In depths of soul within.
> To thee, O Spirit of God,
> Myself I seek in turn
> That strength and grace and skill
> For learning and for work
> In me may live and grow.

The opening line contains the words "I do behold,"

which put an emphasis on the self, on the individuality of each child active in the beholding of the outer world. The mood is a more personal one than in the earlier verse, and we shall see that the curriculum unfolds with a similar mood.

At the request of parents who did not belong to any specific religious denomination, Rudolf Steiner introduced the "independent religion lessons" coupled with a service for children. As the first Waldorf school grew, this was expanded to instruction and services for students of the middle school and high school. Although these lessons and services are held in many Waldorf schools across the world, they are only given at the request of parents in one or two schools on the North American continent.

Yet Rudolf Steiner's syllabus for the religion lessons from the fifth to the eighth grade can serve as a useful guide. In it, Steiner points out that the religion lessons given during these years should help the students understand little by little the workings of the Christ Impulse. In the general curriculum, of course, the teacher does not give religion lessons as such, but he or she does with every lesson create important moods of soul, e.g., attitudes of respect and wonder, feelings of compassion and caring for others and the earth, and a firm path toward ideals. As the religion lessons develop for those students who take them, so, too, are there equivalents to be found in the curriculum as a whole that the teacher can make fruitful for the inner life of the children.

Let us consider a few highlights of the curriculum as given in the main lessons along the lines of the Book of Nature, or Geographia, and the Book of Civilization, or Historia.

Book of Nature **GEOGRAPHIA**	**Book of Civilization** **HISTORIA**

Grade V (Age 11)

Geography (N. America)	Ancient civilizations
Botany	India & Persia
	Egypt & Greece

Grade VI (Age 12)

Geography (Europe)	Rome & Christianity
Mineralogy	Islam
Introduction to the	Middle Ages
sciences	Kalevala
Geometrical drawings	Arthurian tales
	Grail stories

Grade VII (Age 13)

Mechanics	The Birth of the Renaissance
Electricity &	The Explorers
magnetism	Discovering the world
Astronomy	The Birth of the
Nutrition &	scientific age
hygiene	
Geography (other	
continents)	

Grade VIII (Age 14)

Chemistry	Revolution
Physiology	Evolution
World geography	The Wars of Independence
The peoples of Earth,	The French Revolution:
their ways of life,	liberty, equality, fraternity
habits, customs,	The Industrial Revolution
religions, & rituals	(England)
Economics	The Spiritual Revolution
Industry &	(German idealism)
transportation	Contemporary history
	The 20th century

39

Although the above table provides only an overview, it is clear that the curriculum in these four grades has become far more complex than the one followed in the first four grades.

The Curriculum of the Fifth Grade

The fifth grade marks a transition which in the course of a few years will lead the students to adolescence. It marks the birth of the individuality and a growing interest in the world around. The curriculum reflects this transition. In the fifth grade we move from the mythologies of the ancient civilizations to the birth of consciousness of self and logical thought in Greece. The teacher should be aware that the culture and religion of ancient civilizations can be understood as preparation for the Christ event on earth. Krishna, the teacher of Arjuna in the *Bhagavad Gita,* teaches humanity a profound sense of reverence for the Divine. A strict discipline is taught for the one who wishes to unite himself with a universal Godhead. The path is outlined. Later, the teachings of Buddha, the master of compassion, reinforce this approach, and through the practice of the Eight-Fold Path, a soul attitude is prepared for receiving some five hundred years later the message of Christ.

In ancient Persia, the great initiate Zarathustra, the servant of Ahura Mazdao, the Sun Being, brings the gift of agriculture to humanity. The teacher should understand that in Ahura Mazdao we have a reflection of the Cosmic Christ as He gradually approaches the earthly realm.

Another facet of humanity's connection with the spiritual worlds appears in ancient Egyptian civilization in the stories of Isis and Osiris. The emphasis here is not only on whether the activities of human beings on earth are in tune with the gods, but also on the preparation for entering the other world, across the waters, at death when each one will have to face the judgment of Osiris. Ancient Egypt is still able to celebrate the rituals that connect us with the supersensible world. But as the preceding great civilizations eventually decline, Egypt, too, falls into decadence by the time Greece takes up the torch.

Individual biographies become important as the students enter into the glory of Greece in their main lesson. In fact, the recognition of individuality begins with the stories of the Trojan War, when we hear of the exploits of Hector, Cassandra, Agamemnon, Odysseus, and many others who now begin to stand out as individuals with their personal destinies, although still under the inspiration of the gods and goddesses. As history proceeds, the direct connection with the supersensible grows increasingly faint with each civilization. The world after death becomes uncertain, and in ancient Greece the saying, "Better to be a beggar on earth than a king in the realm of the shades," permeates the consciousness of that time.

Whereas Plato was still inspired out of the mysteries, this is no longer true of Aristotle, who fashions thought forms by dint of his own inner activity. The preparation for the Christ event can be seen clearly in the development of Greek thought which is reflected both in the John Gospel and in the writings of St. Paul.

In the study of the Book of Nature we now widen our perspective to the country in which the Waldorf school is situated and to the study of botany, a living consideration

41

of the plant world from the most primitive forms to the flowering species, culminating in the rose and the lily. An immersion in the process of metamorphosis helps the students to develop flexibility in thinking, an enormously important capacity for going beyond the hard, materialistic concepts of our time and for grasping spiritual ideas that can lead to an experience of the Christ Impulse. And quite apart from stimulating an interest in the flora of the world, it also provides them with a more tolerant, broad-minded attitude towards life.

The Curriculum of the Sixth Grade

In preparation for teaching this grade, the teacher can focus in a special way on the Christ Impulse. We shall embark upon the splendors and decadence of the Roman Empire by way of contrasting biographies (in the manner of Plutarch) and describe the birth and rise of Christianity. We shall deal with the life of Jesus Christ from the childhood of Jesus of Nazareth to the birth of the Christ as a result of the baptism in the Jordan. There are many opportunities to deal with the biographies of Matthew, Mark, Luke, and John, of Mary and Veronica and to paint graphic portraits of the opponents, such as Herod, Herodias, and others.

One can contrast the opulence and decadence of Rome with the devoted and frugal life in the catacombs. Christianity lived as a seed under the hard crust of the declining Mysteries. It would be helpful to consider the lives of the twelve Apostles, of their struggles and strivings; Thomas in India, James the Great in Spain, and Andrew in Russia, for example. The life and voyages of St.

Paul might best be left to a later time.

The teacher's course through the Middle Ages would deal with the various orders and their inaugurators, for instance, St. Benedict and St. Francis. One could also deal with some of the heretical groups to show the different facets of a Christianity that was still trying to find itself. The building of the Romanesque and Gothic churches and cathedrals plays a prominent part. People were still naturally religious.

But what characterizes the true Christ Impulse? Wherever deeds of healing, of compassion, of love are found, where human beings sacrifice their own well-being for the well-being of others, that is a manifestation of the Christ Impulse. Our teaching, therefore, must not have anything of a dogmatic nature. We should help the children to see that wherever the Christ Impulse has appeared, it has changed people's lives for the better. Conversely, wherever the Christ Impulse manifests, suppressed hate, distrust, and terror have also reared their heads. The lives of Jacques de Molay and Philip le Bel illustrate this tension in a most dramatic way in the rise and fall of the Templars.

We should remember that in teaching history, especially in a vivid way through biography and bringing a period to life in the classroom, we might well strike a period or certain events that are close to our own destinies and those of the children in a previous incarnation. Walter Johannes Stein told me of a situation that occurred to him in the sixth grade of the first Waldorf school. He was dealing with the life of Charlemagne and his cruel persecution of the Saxons because they rejected the Christ. We recall that he executed those who failed to convert.

The chief of the Saxons, Widukind, finding this incomprehensible, disguised himself and with great courage penetrated into the large tent at Aachen where the midnight Christmas Mass was being celebrated in the presence of Charlemagne and his followers. When the Host was lifted by the priest at the altar, Widukind recognized in it the Sun God which the Saxons also revered. After the celebration, Widukind, throwing off his disguise, embraced Charlemagne and said, "We are brothers. Your Christ Jesus is also our Sun God." This resulted in a momentous reconciliation, as can well be imagined.

Walter Johannes Stein told his class this story in his most dramatic fashion, and when he came to the end, the whole class stood up in silence—an impressive moment, indeed.

Now Stein repeated this story to another sixth grade a year later (the class teacher arrangement was not yet complete). On this occasion, although the children seemed moved, they did not stand up. Stein approached Rudolf Steiner and asked him whether he could throw light on the difference. Rudolf Steiner said to him, "You see the students of the first sixth grade were there in a previous incarnation, whereas those in the second sixth grade, although also reincarnated at that time, only heard about it."

This is a rather wonderful example that will help us to treat the teaching of history in a very sensitive and subtle way, bearing in mind that we touch upon many karmic strands that have been woven in the past and now reappear in the classroom.

As in history so also in the introduction to the sciences,

much can be done through biography. The lives of the great inventors often show that their achievements are the results of a strong spiritual guidance.

A special opportunity is given in the block on acoustics and optics. We are dealing with hearing and seeing, the two principal organs for discovering the physical world around us. Steiner said that the old breathing yoga of the Hindus is today metamorphosed in the yoga of the senses. We should not only learn to hear and to see clearly, but to sense the spirit weaving in the material world that we apprehend through our sense organs. This is also a path to the Christ Being.

The Curriculum of the Seventh Grade

In this overview, history at the beginning of the seventh grade plays a special role. We are at the dawn of the consciousness soul in the early part of the fifteenth century. Two figures stand out. One is Joan of Arc in France who, inspired at an early age by St. Michael and permeated by the Christ Impulse, brings about the separation of France and England. The formation of nations, each with its own language, takes on a special importance in the development of western humanity. The other figure is Jan Hus, the powerful religious reformer from Prague who, like Joan, died the ignoble death of being burned at the stake, he at the Lake of Constance. They both offered the ultimate sacrifice in order to help the evolution of the individual and of mankind forward.

The whole of the Renaissance stands under the sign of crossing new frontiers in the arts and sciences and through the amazing exploits of the navigators. Here biographies abound. The lives of Leonardo da Vinci, Raphael, and Michelangelo stand out, not only as great painters, architects, and sculptors of the age, but also as those who strove to embody aspects of the Christ Impulse in their works. It is interesting to compare them to the northern trinity of Dürer, Bosch, and Grünewald. The anti-forces of the Borgia pope formed a fearful contrast to the benevolent powers that were seeking to emerge.

One will certainly not fail to bring the lives of Henry the Navigator, Christopher Columbus, and others who sailed forth under the guidance of the Order of Christ, a stream resurrected in Portugal by Prince Henry after the destruction of the Templars. Whatever happened later, we should remember that all the great voyages of discovery were made in the true name of Christ. That they became decadent subsequently is one of the great tragedies of history, leading to the most abject suppression of people.

The geography curriculum will help us greatly in getting to know the customs and the way of life of many distant people. We will have learned earlier of the travels of Marco Polo and gained insight into the marvelous culture of the Chinese, but we shall also discover India with its rich spiritual traditions, Japan, and other parts of the Orient.

The consciousness soul cannot be developed without mankind having discovered the whole of the earth in all its diversity of flora, fauna, and civilizations. This, too, is a profound pilgrimage towards understanding the workings of Christ, the Sun God, who came for all peoples. The other pole is the development of the individual which occurs through many trials and tribulations.

46

It should be emphasized that these indications are merely suggestions by means of which we can begin to perceive the general tenor of these four grades against the background of the Christ Impulse in the broadest sense. It can never be a question of dogmatic pronouncements or rigid conclusions.

This is one of the fundamental reasons why we teach history through biography. These studies are made all the more vivid if we choose contrasting life stories to illustrate a particular period. Much can be gained by comparing and contrasting, for instance, the following: Washington and Jefferson, Abraham Lincoln and John Brown, Elizabeth I and Mary Queen of Scots, Johannes Kepler (the astronomer who, because of his shortsightedness, could hardly see the stars, but displayed a genius for mathematics) and Tycho de Brahe (the Danish astronomer who charted the heavenly bodies with extraordinary accuracy out of observation).

As a further example one might mention the two architects of the modern French language who lived in the seventeenth century, Blaise Pascal and René Descartes, both mathematicians. In Pascal we have a deeply religious man who suffered from the most excruciating headaches and accomplished so much in mathematics and physics by dint of extraordinary endurance. Descartes, a physician, also renowned for his mathematical genius, promulgated the conviction that the different organs of the human being were really parts of a machine, thus paving the way for the concept of man as a machine. While they knew one another and held similar interests, they followed very different spiritual paths.

These are but a few suggestions. Individual teachers will readily discover a host of other fruitful examples. In circles of Waldorf teachers, Herbert Hahn was a forerunner in the field of contrasting biographies and during his long years as a teacher in the first Waldorf school he chose such individualities as Verdi and Tolstoy, Champollion (the nineteenth century scholar, the first in our modern world to penetrate the mysteries of the ancient Egyptian hieroglyphics by means of the Rosetta Stone), and Schliemann (the archeologist who discovered ancient Troy).

The Curriculum of the Eighth Grade

The curriculum of the eighth grade is very much guided by the activity of widening our horizons into a worldwide view of the peoples of the earth. Through the study of geography we develop a greater understanding of the family of mankind in its extraordinary diversity of peoples and habitats. With chemistry, physiology, and electricity we probe more deeply into the mysteries of life on earth. We learn to understand the laws of nature, yet also maintain a sense of wonder at what scientific investigation can reveal to us.

The history curriculum focuses more and more on contemporary social conditions—after a lively consideration, still by way of the lives of great men and women, of the various revolutions that occurred during the last few centuries. Emphasis would be placed on American history, on the wars of independence, and the founding fathers and their high ideals, on a nation founded on Christian ideals, practical, yet also filled with idealism and hope for the future. These ideals drew people from all over the world, hoping that what lived in them individually would be given an opportunity to unfold in a better, more meaningful life in freedom. Such figures as Washington and Jefferson, Benjamin Franklin and Lafayette could be dramatically contrasted to paint a picture of the times.

Around 1800, which in many ways heralds the tensions that we find in our own time, one can clearly detect three principal revolutions. The French Revolution that began in the euphoria of bright ideals ended in a reign of terror. Thousands of people were sacrificed to bring about the ideal of equality which failed lamentably. In England the emphasis was on an industrial revolution that herded countless men, women, and children into the factories and textile mills, depleting agricultural communities which were still living with the beauties and rhythms of nature. The ideal of fraternity (brotherhood and sisterhood) was often sullied by ruthless exploitation. Yet, there were also powerful reformers often risking their own careers in order to transform a widely corrupt system. William Wilberforce, the British reform politician who sponsored the passage of a bill abolishing slave trade, and Robert Owen, the great British social reformer who established in Scotland a model industrial community with good housing and working conditions, nursery schools, and cooperative shops, stand out for their tireless effort. Later, Robert Owen attempted to establish similar conditions in a community in the United States.

In this context we shall be able to draw strongly on the works of Charles Dickens. *A Tale of Two Cities* will offer rich and dramatic panoramas of London and Paris during the French Revolution, but more important will be the many works where Dickens deals with child exploitation, the suppression and neglect of the poor, and the incredible corruption of an unjust legal system. Dickens did more through the genius of his writings to awaken public consciousness to the evils of the times than any other in Britain. His stories are not only heartrending and can literally bring the reader to tears, but at every turn his incredible sense of fun and humor shines through, redeeming the gloom. At this stage in the life of the students, his *A Christmas Carol* should not only be read but might also be presented as a play. The story is a profoundly esoteric one and weaves between existence on the physical plane and life after death. It centers around the dark, miserly Scrooge and the radiant innocence of Tiny Tim. It is no coincidence that Scrooge's transformation, bringing joy and well-being to all around him, takes place during the Christmas season.

Regarding contrasting biographies, we might well compare the life of Charles Dickens with that of Victor Hugo. An interesting bridge can thereby be built between Britain and France by two men who labored incessantly for social reform and actually met on one occasion. The story of *Les Misérables* should definitely be included at this time.

The third revolution, around and after 1800, took place in middle Europe. There we find the call to freedom ringing out in the music of Beethoven, the dramas of Schiller, and the early works of Goethe. *"Sturm und Drang"* (Storm and Stress) are the order of the day, and though no outward battles were fought, the inner upheavals were mighty. How could humanity reach the noble ideal of

"Freiheit" (although it means freedom, the German includes a connotation of spiritual independence)? Aspects of these artists' biographies can be brought. One might also compare the works of Mozart and Beethoven—the breaking of conventions and tight structures. In an English-speaking world it might be more difficult to deal with the great representatives of German idealism, who largely functioned as the philosophers of a great renewal, Hegel, Schelling, and Fichte.

During the course of the seventh and eighth grades, one might also give assignments of a biographical nature to the students, stimulating their own research. Their findings could then be presented orally to the whole class and in written form later. It can lead to lively discussion. A list of biographies chosen by the teacher might include a number of individualities who have played an important part in the service of humanity in alleviating the social misery of their time. The following come to mind:

Florence Nightingale (selfless pioneer of the nursing profession)

Clara Barton (philanthropist, deeply involved in caring for the sick)

Pestalozzi (Swiss pioneer educator, caring especially for poor and orphan children)

Henri Dunant (Swiss philanthropist, founder of the Red Cross, having shared the horrifying conditions of the wounded in several conflicts)

Albert Schweitzer (Alsatian musician, theologian, physician, missionary to Africa, who birthed the concept of "reverence for life")

Antoine de St. Exupéry (poet, pioneer aviator, who sought to bring peoples of different nations and races together)

The above individualities—and many others could be added—embody the Christ Impulse through their deeds of healing, self-sacrifice, and service to a greater cause. Such considerations will inspire youngsters at this age with genuine idealism.

One further thought: In dealing with biographies at this stage we should begin to draw attention to the weaving of destiny (karma) that constantly lives between people; how one person affects another, how joys and sorrows are shared through the intertwining relationships. Many fruitful vistas can be discovered in studying the biographies of Emerson and Thoreau who were so different even in their approach to life, yet stimulated one another in a remarkable way. Striking examples can be found in the destinies of Stanley and Livingston and the exploration of Africa. One feels that these men knew one another even before they ever met.

Adventure stories on the high seas should also not be neglected. Dramatic examples are found in the works of Melville and Joseph Conrad. The students should get a feel for the fact that there is no "chance encounter," but that every meeting between human beings has a deeper significance which might not necessarily reveal itself at first sight. Finally, there comes to mind the heartrending stories by the great Russians, Tolstoy, Lesskow, and Pushkin which illustrate the dramatic struggle of the human being between his sensual and angelic natures.

Teachers would do well to reflect upon the indication that Steiner gave in 1911 in a course of lectures entitled *From Jesus to Christ*, where he said that the Christ has now become the Lord of Karma, whereas previously

Moses held that office. The law of Moses was "an eye for an eye and a tooth for a tooth." Through the Christ we can learn forgiveness and healing, and He ministers so that in the course of future incarnations we might learn to compensate for the misdeeds of the past.

Each subject that we teach develops specific faculties in the children in addition to the knowledge thereby acquired. It is helpful to recall as a background that the teaching of geography cultivates a sense of gratitude for everything that we find on earth. History quickens a sense of self in the children through their learning about the different civilizations and changing conditions of consciousness. Geography brings about a sense of responsibility for the earth; history reveals the meaning of our own destiny. This might also help us to gain an understanding of the background of the Christ Impulse out of which we are seeking to teach.

Chapter V

The Attitude of the High School Teacher

From the preceding chapters we have seen that much in Waldorf education depends on the inner attitude of the teacher. This inner attitude not only is of importance in the early grades, but also plays a central role in how and what we teach in the high school. Teens are especially sensitive to their teachers' moods of soul. And with children of all ages, these moods permeate the classroom around and through whatever subject is being presented. This entire matter is difficult to describe. It is, in a sense, "imponderable;" it cannot be reproduced outwardly.

How then might a teacher work with it in a way that is beneficial for the students? One way to create a mood in oneself that can properly nurture one's students is by repeatedly and actively contemplating the following key phrases Rudolf Steiner has given us:

Education should be *nurturing* for young children.
Education should be *enlivening* in the middle grades.
Education should be *awakening* in the high school
years.

This *nurturing* aspect of education reminds us once again that in the early grades we teach out of the Father and Mother forces of creation. In the later grades, the *enlivening* element is quickened through the presence of the Christ Impulse. In the high school years, the *awakening* dimension calls for the creative activity of the Holy Spirit.

It makes a radical difference in what occurs in the classroom—whether or not the teacher is aware of these three principles and strives to the best of his or her ability to bring these "imponderables" to expression in the classroom.

If we seek to work out of the New Mysteries as described by Rudolf Steiner, the first step is to understand what a meditation implies. The next is to learn to permeate our heart, our feeling life, with its content and then gradually to make it active in our deeds. The path is usually from an enlivened thinking that leads to Imagination, to balanced feeling that touches Inspiration, and to a firm, strong will that gives birth to Intuition. Teachers can gain a great deal by turning again and again to passages in *Knowledge of Higher Worlds and Its Attainment*, a book that outlines a path of individual development suited to the modern, western mind trained in the scientific discipline of our age.

What Is the Nature of the Holy Spirit?

For our look into high school teaching, we must turn to an understanding of the Holy Spirit. Of course, we cannot pedantically assign the forces of the Father and Mother to the first four grades alone. They continue throughout all of the grades. The same applies to the Christ Impulse.

For instance, in the fifth grade when we are dealing with Greek mythology, Zeus represents a powerful Father element, and Demeter is the finest expression of the Earth Mother. It is also helpful if the teacher understands that in Dionysos is found a forerunner of the Christ. The teacher will discover a number of such relationships while studying ancient India, Egypt, and other early world cultures. Clearly the Christ Impulse also flows in the high school, in history, in biography, in the arts.

Let us now try to understand more closely the workings of the Holy Spirit. If we consider the three main Christian festivals of the year, we find that Christmas, connected with the miracle of birth, is a gift from the Father and Mother ground of worlds. At the Christmas season we can experience that "we are born out of God," which in the Middle Ages was referred to with the Latin words: "*Ex Deo Nascimur,*" meaning "Out of God we are born."

The Easter time of year focuses on the life, death, and resurrection of Christ Jesus. Again in the Middle Ages, out of a profound Rosicrucian tradition, appears the expression: "*In Christo Morimur,*" meaning "In Christ, death becomes life."

The mood of Pentecost (also known as Whitsun), celebrated fifty days after Easter, is very different. The twelve disciples (Judas has been replaced by Matthias) together with Mary Sophia (the Mother) gather in silent expectation after having lost for the last ten days (that is, between Ascension and Whitsun) all connection with the Christ. *The Acts of the Apostles* by Luke describes the dramatic event:

> Suddenly a sound like the blowing of a violent wind came from heaven and filled the whole house where they were sitting. They saw what seemed to be tongues of fire that separated and came to rest on each of them. All were filled with the Holy Spirit and began to speak in other tongues as the Spirit enabled them. (Acts 2:1-5)

57

The Christ had sent them the Comforter, the Holy Spirit, that quickens the individual and can be experienced in true community-forming. It is a Spirit that changes each individual out of its fire forces, yet brings everyone together in a new way. In the Middle Ages, the phrase that arose for this was: *"Per Spiritum Sanctum Reviviscimus,"* meaning "We are re-enlivened out of the Spirit."

It should be mentioned that another name for the Holy Spirit is the Sophia, the spiritual source of wisdom and enlightenment. This third person of the Trinity was always viewed as feminine in nature, until that reality became obscured from the fifteenth century onward. In ancient mythology, reflections of the Holy Sophia are found in Isis of the Egyptians, Kwan Yin of the Chinese, Kanon of the Japanese, and Pallas Athena of the Greeks. These goddesses played momentous roles in the past. Now the time has come to recognize their importance again in the affairs of human beings on the earth. The appearances of Mary in Yugoslavia and Portugal to groups of children may well be connected with the renewed interest.

What then is the aim of the subjects taught in the high school? Whether in the humanities, sciences, or artistic activities, the aim is that the teaching of these subjects quickens the hearts and minds of the students and brings them together in an experience of community.

Let us illustrate the process by taking the instance of producing a play with students of the twelfth grade. A Shakespeare play has been chosen (possibly after considerable debate). The parts have been given and volunteers have been found to see to the costumes, work the lights, and do the publicity. Yet there are still quite a few rumblings among the members of the class. The usual dissatisfactions rear their ugly heads: petty jealousies, ambitions, and the like. The rehearsals begin: some find it difficult to learn their lines, others rattle them off thoughtlessly. Patience, perseverance, and tolerance are needed by all.

While these weeks of preparation can be quite trying, they offer an excellent exercise in social interaction, in learning, for instance, to appreciate the strong points in one another and to overcome one's own weaknesses for the sake of a production to be performed for parents and friends and perhaps for members of the community at large.

Gradually the rehearsals take shape with music and eurythmy. The sets are painted by an eager, creative crew. We begin to witness a cheerful give and take in the face of last minute difficulties. The opening night has arrived; anticipation and stage fright fill the air. "Will we succeed?" The play unfolds, the first moments of hesitation have been dispelled; as if by "miracle" a mood of togetherness descends over the whole company. It is palatable by all; the audience too feels it. Something has happened that is more than the effort of each student to do his or her best. At that moment a community experience arises that brings everyone together in a new and unexpected way. It may not last long, it cannot be reproduced at will, but it will be remembered as a creative, unique moment where something more happened than was planned. It is a moment of grace quickened by the Spirit. Looking back, we might become aware that it was a great deal more than having had a successful performance.

It is true that such moments happen whether or not the teacher cultivates an inner attitude of conscious working with the Holy Spirit. However, the teacher who does cultivate such an attitude is warmly inviting such moments to enter into the classes being taught and perhaps will more readily recognize such moments when they do occur.

A Few General Considerations

To develop our theme in connection with the high school presents us with a number of difficulties. In the first place one should consider the psychological makeup of the students through these four grades. The changes through which they go inwardly and outwardly are very rapid and decisive. Whereas the ninth grader is still turbulent, unfocused, and little in control of himself or herself, the twelfth grader usually shows considerable balance and self-reliance and the beginnings of a sound sense of being able to cope with life.

It would go far beyond the framework of this chapter to deal with these rapid and incisive changes. Nevertheless, we can see clearly from the curriculum in the humanities, sciences, history of art, and the artistic and practical activities, that each of the four high school grades has a specific character intending to meet the students at their particular stage of development.

The Gesture of the Ninth Grade

Every attempt should be made to teach the various blocks out of a consideration of the "phenomenon." In other words, the high school teacher teaches through observation and participation in preference to explanation.

Rudolf Steiner indicated that learning "to know" was of special importance at this stage. In the ninth grade the emphasis also is on things modern and contemporary, such as the study of history and physics. Communication and transportation play a major part in the studies. The great inventions and scientific discoveries should be underlined. The achievements of James Watt, Edison, Marconi, Faraday, and many others will provide a backbone to the deeper study of physics.

It is in such studies, surprisingly enough, that we can also clearly detect the workings of the Spirit. It is truly amazing, for instance, how the microscope and the telescope were developed. Most inventions were sparked by a sudden inspiration. Often, they also arose out of a dream or upon awakening in the morning. The "eureka" of Archimedes has been repeated a thousandfold through human history. These indeed are sparks of the Spirit. Whether their applications have been used for good or evil is another matter, but one can see clearly that certain inventions needed to be made as part of the development of mankind.

A history of the visual arts from ancient Egypt to Rembrandt forms a predominant part of this grade's work. It leads us from a collective, almost dreamlike consciousness of large masses guided by initiated pharaohs to the marked individuality of a Rembrandt. The scope of these blocks (possibly two three-week blocks in the course of the year) is considerable. It takes us from the pyramids and temples of Egypt to the Golden Age of Greece with its remarkable statues of gods and goddesses, to the Early Christian basilica, from the primitive Italian and Flemish masters to the Renaissance when perspective emerged and the golden background gave way to a representation of the individual in his or her own right. Through the history of art we see a move from the sacred to the secular. Particularly in Holland, the emerging bourgeoisie became the proud possessors of paintings and portraits representing everyday life. Rembrandt represents a culmination. He deals with both the sacred and the secular, adding a new dimension by painting, sketching, and etching over a hundred self-portraits during a period of forty-two years, from the time he was twenty-one to his death at sixty-three. His is a quest for the true "I am."

This indeed will fascinate the teenagers—discovering through beauty and the changing times the varied, innovative gifts of the great masters. For instance, how different is a Leonardo da Vinci from a Raphael, or a Dürer from a Michelangelo? In them all, one discovers an innovative, original principle that touches upon the often mysterious workings of the Holy Spirit. The genius of a great master is characterized by his ability to embody a profound inspiration and make it visible (or audible, in the case of music) to countless human beings throughout the ages. It is on this ever-renewing process that our culture is based.

In the geography block special attention will be given to geology (which signifies "earth meaning"). The mountain cross of the folded ranges clearly inscribed in north-south and east-west directions across the globe is a remarkable feature, especially when we consider that Plato said that the soul of the world is crucified on the cross of the earth.

The geology of everyday things is also of interest. For instance, the ripening of camembert cheese and the making of champagne wine (from the Champagne region of France) depend on the particular properties of limestone caves; the specific quality of English woolens is the result of washing and shrinking processes with waters flowing over the Millstone grit, a sandstone found in the heart of the English countryside. Over all, no opportunity should be missed to discover the "lawfulness" in the abundant wisdom of nature.

The ninth grader who awakens to a new sense of idealism should be helped through the curriculum to "wonder" at the many mysteries of life that surround us, and of which we are an integral part. Presenting the phenomena in a lively way without preconceived notions is critical at this stage. Here, too, much will depend on the teacher: Can he or she genuinely live with the mysteries of life? The teacher dealing with ninth grade students may find that reflecting on the thought and attitudes of Goethe toward nature can be of great inspiration.

The Gesture of the Tenth Grade

This particular phase in life is a search for inner and outer balance. The subjects therefore deal with resolving polarities in the earth structure; for instance, in the balance between the four elements of earth, air, water, and fire, as they express themselves in meteorology and climate. We should endeavor to show that the earth is a living organism. Mankind as a whole, and each individual, bears a responsibility for its further evolution. We do not merely participate. We are called upon to be creative in the workings of the kingdoms of nature: minerals, plants, and animals. Novalis, the sensitive German romantic poet, who died at the early age of twenty-eight, expressed it concisely in one of his many aphorisms: "We are engaged in a mission: we are called upon to fashion, to form, the earth."

It is also the time for studying the living word—the diversity in languages, the idioms and ways of speech of different peoples—and tracing the development of the word through song, poetry, and prose, learning to differentiate between dramatic, epic, and lyrical elements. The balance between consonants and vowels in different languages, such as English, Spanish, French, and German, possibly with examples from Greek, Latin, and Hebrew, would enrich the students' considerations.

The working of the creative spirit can clearly be seen in the molding of language by great poets such as Chaucer and Shakespeare, and in modern times T. S. Eliot, Dylan Thomas, and others. Language is not static. Poets, writers, and speakers of genius contribute to the powerful flow of expression through the word, bringing often surprising facets to the experience of the human soul.

Two examples are given here to illustrate the innovative spirit born of genius in the fashioning of the English language in our own century.

The American-born British poet T. S. Eliot (1888–1965) contributed much by way of plays and poetry to revive the English language during the first half of the century. "Little Gidding," the fourth of the Four Quartets, composed during the Second World War, exemplifies a marked change of consciousness expressed in startling new terms.

The dove descending breaks the air
With flame of incandescent terror
Of which the tongues declare
The one discharge from sin and error.
The only hope, or else despair
  Lies in the Choice of pyre or pyre—
  To be redeemed from fire by fire.

  Who then devised the torment? Love.
Love is the unfamiliar Name
Behind the hands that wove
The intolerable shirt of flame
Which human power cannot remove.
  We only live, only suspire
  Consumed by either fire or fire.

A very different voice is heard in the works of the
Welsh poet Dylan Thomas who died at the early age of
thirty-nine. An anthology of modern poetry, edited by
Oscar Williams (Pocket Books Inc., New York), is
"dedicated to the memory of Dylan Thomas (1914–1953),
major poet, great man and immortal soul."

An extract from "Fern Hill," where the poet gives us a
vivid picture of his youth in Wales, well illustrates his
remarkable facility. His poetic genius broke totally new
ground by enlivening the English language.

Now as I was young and easy under the apple
        boughs
About the lilting house and happy as the grass was
        green,
    The night above the dingle starry,
        Time let me hail and climb
    Golden in the heydays of his eyes,
And honoured among wagons I was prince of the
        apple towns
And once below a time I lordly had the trees and
        leaves

Trail with daisies and barley
Down the rivers of the windfall light.

And as I was green and carefree, famous among the
barns
About the happy yard and singing as the farm was
home,
In the sun that is young once only.
Time let me play and be
Golden in the mercy of his means,
And green and golden I was huntsman and herds-
man, the calves
Sang to my horn, the foxes on the hills barked clear
and cold,
And the sabbath rang slowly
In the pebbles of the holy streams.

The contrast between these two poets is inescapable. In T. S. Eliot we find an Apollonian spirit struggling for rigor and precision guided by the light of measure and meaning. In Dylan Thomas we discover a boisterous, youthful, Dionysian element breaking conventional bounds with a whirlwind of images and invocations.

Many other powerful examples can readily be found in modern English and American literature. It belongs to the tenth grade to engage the students in an appreciation of the word, of the logos through its manifold expressions.

A great deal more could be said in connection with the other blocks of this year, such as chemistry, mathematics, ancient history, and so on. In them all, the same principle of balance will be discerned.

The Gesture of the Eleventh Grade

This year stands under the sign of the "question" and the "quest." The Parsifal story is paramount: the pure fool, who fails to ask the question in the presence of the wounded King Amfortas, upon his first visit to the Grail Castle. The complex saga as related by Wolfram von Eschenbach, with more than two hundred characters, depicts Parsifal in his many adventures going through dullness and doubt before attaining, as a result of great suffering, a stage of blessedness where he can ask a question, heal the ailing Amfortas, and become the new Grail King.

It is a poignant story of awakening to the higher self out of the darkness and dimness of one's lower being. It is remarkably appropriate for teenagers at this stage of life and points dramatically to how spiritual renewal can lead to a sense of community.

In contrast, study in the eleventh grade also takes the students on a journey toward understanding the more hidden forces of nature: the cathode ray tube and nuclear energy will be investigated, and steps are taken toward fathoming the riddles of matter.

Special consideration will also be given during this year to the development of music, the most elusive of the arts, for it is not tangible like architecture, sculpture, and painting, which are present in space. In music a threshold is crossed. Music develops in time; the spacial element is virtually absent.

We started in the high school with the history of the visual arts—learning to see. In the tenth grade we moved to the living word—learning to hear and understand. In the eleventh grade we find that the history of music teaches us to hear in a deeper way, beyond the word; this deeper listening is accessible to the whole of mankind.

The creative spirit lives and moves in new ways as we study the composers. We may be astonished at the manner in which they were inspired, and at how different the nature of inspiration is in a Mozart from a Beethoven, in a Bartok from a Stravinsky. Many composers testified to something higher working in or through them. Their genius consisted in the final forming, but the origin lies in the divine inspiration they were able to receive.

We are indeed, in this grade, dealing with many "imponderables." This is further reflected in the mathematics and geometry curriculum as we move into calculus and projective geometry, and into the mysteries of the study of botany. A consideration of Shakespeare's *Hamlet*, particularly his grappling with the meaning of life in the famous "To be or not to be" monologue, will touch the students deeply. How can doubt be overcome? How can we find truth, not in an abstract, fixed way, but as a process, a quest that has to be undertaken again and again? This indeed presents a poignant, existential path. In this light, appropriate are the words of Christ Jesus, prophesying the manner in which He would send the Holy Spirit, the Comforter: "You will know the truth and the truth will make you free."

The Gesture of the Twelfth Grade

The treatment of all the subjects in this grade stands under the concept of "synthesis," a bringing together, a gathering of all the topics that have been studied previously, adding a deeper element in tune with the maturing student.

Although the form of the "round table" will be

introduced in the seating arrangement on a number of occasions from the tenth grade onwards, in the twelfth grade it becomes of paramount importance. Every effort will be made so that the students can present assignments to one another, first orally and then in writing, and we should engage in much conversation to solve the particular questions that are raised. It is astonishing what can happen in this way and how often something totally new can arise through the interplay, which can even surprise us as teachers. Is this not the mark of the Holy Spirit that weaves between us in a healing, harmonizing manner?

The emphasis in this grade lies in the overview: world geography is taught from the point of view of world economy; world history is treated as symptomatology which would include historical perceptives of Africa, Asia, South America, Australia, etc.; and world religions are presented in an overview of the beliefs of Islam, Hinduism, Buddhism, Judaism, and the various Christian denominations. (Here an attempt will also be made to consider the heretical Christian streams, such as the Cathars and the Bogomils.)

We will also study *Faust*, Parts I and II, by Goethe. It is a unique work of art which took Goethe no less than sixty years to complete. The first sketches were begun when he was twenty-one, and shortly before his death at the age of eighty-three he sealed Part II, leaving strict instructions that the work should be published only after his death.

The range of this work alone is stupendous. The "Prologue in Heaven" tells us, in accordance with the Book of Job, that God the Father allowed the devil to tempt humanity, but that the Lord God, in spite of humanity's errings, has unshakable confidence in the human being remaining faithful to the Divine and finding his way to God again. Much profound discussion can take place, quickened by this Prologue, on the question of evil. It will lead quite naturally to other themes for discussion in *Faust*, such as the "Gretchen tragedy," the nature of lust in Faust's determination to seduce a young, innocent maiden; the effects of drugs and alcohol; questions of suicide, death, and immortality.

The complex topic of redemption also plays an important part, for towards the end of the second part of *Faust* we hear that whoever strives continually can be redeemed. These considerations move the students deeply and lead to many discussions. Depending on the teacher, other great works of American, English, and foreign literature might be introduced, such as the Russian masterpiece *The Brothers Karamazov* by Dostoyevsky, where the basest and the noblest aspirations in the human being are depicted with such heartrending, dramatic power.

In the study of Victor Hugo's *Les Misérables*, another facet of the wealth of European literature can enthuse the students. Highlights in German, Russian, and French literature can also spark an interest in the different ways of life of the peoples in accordance with their folk souls. Further excursions could be made into the Haiku poems of the Japanese and Japanese ways of life, customs, and rituals.

The sciences will of course not be neglected. And there again, by considering biographies in chemistry, physics, zoology, and history of science, the teacher can provide an overview without falling into superficiality.

In fact, this is perhaps one of the greatest challenges in the high school. How can we, considering the abundance of facts and subjects, learn to teach economically? It means making a careful choice, bringing out highlights in such a way that they quicken the student in wanting to learn more in his or her own time. Surely the most important thing is that through our teaching and guidance the youngster will want to explore and deepen.

Outstanding individualities of our own century can also be dealt with. The remarkable life of Dag Hammarskjöld, who as Secretary General of the United Nations (1953–1965) revealed a profound hidden side to his nature in *Markings*, and the impulse of Simone Weil, the French mystic of Jewish background, could also be studied. Attracted to Christianity, Weil took up work as a factory hand in the Midlands of England during the Second World War out of a deep longing to serve and share in the hard destiny of the working classes. Her written works include *Waiting for God*, a poignant statement of the modern alienated soul striving to find its roots. No less interesting are the lives of the Dalai Lama and Mother Theresa.

A global view of the history of architecture, in studying forms, proportions, and materials, will help students understand the sacred and the secular lives of peoples all over the world. This will also help in grasping different stages of consciousness as they reveal themselves, for instance, in the Egyptian pyramids, the Greek temples, the Early Christian basilicas, and the Romanesque and Gothic cathedrals. In seeking to understand the original rituals of the Hindus, the Chinese, and the Japanese, a study of their temples can be most rewarding. Aphorisms by men and

71

women who have made a positive impact on the affairs of the world can also be presented for discussion or offer themes for essays. Three instances could be quoted, the first by Leo Tolstoy:

> Man is not alone on the chessboard of life. He is surrounded by divine powers, Love and Wisdom and all the good forces of providence in this world of shadows and light.

The second, an extract from a letter by Vincent van Gogh to his brother Theo:

> I feel with all my strength that the history of mankind follows the same course as that of wheat. All is useless unless we are sown into the earth in order to burst forth into flower. We shall be ground in order to turn into bread.

The third, a passage from the Gospel of St. John (12:24):

> Verily, verily, I say unto you, unless a seed falls into the earth and dies, it remains alone. But if it dies, it bears much fruit. Who loves his own soul, will lose it; but he who hates that which passes, will preserve his soul for life eternal.

The plenitude of considerations as they arise out of the varied spectrum of the twelfth grade curriculum is intended to awaken the students to their own innermost selves and quicken their sense of how, as growing adults, they can best serve their fellow human beings. Not so long ago one spoke in terms of finding one's "vocation" or "calling." Interestingly enough, both words are related to hearing. When we find our task in life, we have heard what speaks out of the deepest recesses of our own heart and mind. Not to find one's calling, one's destiny, is one of the greatest tragedies in our age of alienation.

In conclusion, it should be pointed out that the students of the twelfth grade should have ample opportunity for discussing two topics: one is the social question and the other is the necessity of the modern human being to face evil. Naturally this can be done in many ways. One might deal, for example, with the ideals of the French Revolution, "freedom, equality, and fraternity," and consider how these are still relevant in our time. How much has been achieved in the last two hundred years and what has still to be done now and in the future? To what extent is there freedom in the religious, cultural, and educational sphere of society? Is there equality in the rights and legal realm? Where has brotherliness or fraternity been achieved in the economic sphere?

Walter Johannes Stein once advised me to deal with the social question out of a presentation of world economy in the geography blocks. This could be practiced in our high schools to good effect.

The question of evil will come up in twelfth grade literature class in a discussion of Goethe's *Faust*. Mephistopheles, the evil deceiver, has both a Luciferic and an Ahrimanic side. Although Goethe was unable to differentiate clearly between the two polarities in this figure, nevertheless, by intuition he recommended that Mephistopheles be dressed in Luciferic red in Part I, and in Ahrimanic black in Part II. This can lead the way for the teacher to introduce Lucifer and Ahriman as the double face of evil and show how the good, the golden mean, is found in balance between them. This balance can represent the Christ Impulse and is depicted artistically in Rudolf

Steiner's giant wooden sculpture, some thirty feet in height. It is clearly indicated that the central figure, the Representative of Man or the Christ, is striding, which suggests that the balance between the two extreme forces, the one that wishes to lure us away from physical reality (Lucifer), and the other who seeks to shackle us to matter (Ahriman), needs to be held through constant striving in equilibrium.

Depending on the make-up of the class, one might introduce one of the works of Vladimir Soloviev, Russian mystic, who died in 1900 at the age of forty-seven, and who towards the end of his life wrote, in the form of dialogues, a challenging book entitled, *War and Christianity from the Christian Point of View*. The conversations end with a short story of the Anti-Christ. It shows the rise of the Anti-Christ and how he is overcome by Christian forces. It ends with a triumphant vision of the woman clothed in the sun, with a crown of stars upon her head, and standing on the crescent moon as depicted by St. John the Evangelist in *Revelation*, Chapter 12.

During his lifetime, Soloviev had three powerful experiences of Mary Sophia. The first was at the age of nine during a service in a church in Moscow; later as a young man in the Reading Room of the British Museum, London; and finally at the foot of the pyramids in Egypt. It is undeniable that these three experiences inspired him, shortly before his death, to write the dramatic story of humanity confronting the Anti-Christ.

In teaching in high schools, both in Europe and the United States, I have always found much inspiration for the preparation of lessons in two meditative sentences given by

Rudolf Steiner in a lecture on 24 September, 1919, shortly after the founding of the first Waldorf school:

> Seek real practical life, but seek it in such a way that the spirit which dwells within it is not deadened for you.

And:

> Seek the spirit, but not with supersensible lust, not out of supersensible egoism, but seek it so that you can apply it selflessly in practical life in the material world.

Chapter VI

The Annual Waldorf Teachers' Conference held in Spring Valley in June 1993 was devoted to the theme, "The Christ-Centered Impulse in Waldorf Education." I gave five keynote lectures during the conference, each heard by the more than three hundred practicing Waldorf teachers in attendance.

The first lecture, held on 22 June, was given to the Pedagogical Section. Its members are Waldorf teachers and administrators who are also members of the First Class of the School of Spiritual Science. The content of the opening lecture is here reproduced.

It is with considerable trepidation that I embark upon this theme because in our day and age the very title could lead to serious misunderstandings. On the one hand, we must avoid all dogmatism. On the other hand, it would be a grave error to imply that Waldorf education has little or nothing to do with the Christ Impulse. It belongs to the times that we live in that nothing can be taken for granted, nothing is self-evident, and everything of a spiritual, pedagogical nature has to be re-examined in the light of a new, emerging consciousness.

Teachers are often asked if Waldorf schools are Christian, and even so simple and direct a question cannot be answered by a brief "yes" or "no." If the inquirer is thinking in terms of sectarian Christianity—in some sense denominational—then the answer is "no." If, on the other hand, the question is asked in connection with the deeper aspects of Christianity, an answer might be "yes." Waldorf education as it arises out of Anthroposophy is, in its very nature, a Cosmic Christ-centered impulse. This impulse is expressed implicitly, not explicitly, in our work with the children in the classroom.

Examining One's Own Background

We shall have to travel a long and arduous road in order to gain what may be a new understanding of our essential tasks as teachers. When we survey the troublesome and painful aspects of the world situation and of the personal anguish that has become the destiny of millions, we might say that, indeed, we are entering ever more deeply into a phase of world history that can be characterized as "the descent into hell." In the calendar of the Gospels, Maundy Saturday is preceded by the Last Supper and the Crucifixion. The descent into hell, which is not recorded in the Gospels, may be characterized as the silent Saturday before the renewing light of Resurrection Sunday.

The significance of this descent can be looked upon in different ways: It means coming to terms with that which heretofore was hidden, was unpleasant, was so distasteful that a tabu was cast upon it. To take this downward step means to develop spiritual courage which enables us to face squarely things that have been lying unattended beneath the surface.

In our context, a beginning can be made by asking three fundamental questions:

1. What is my relationship to the Cosmic Christ Impulse?

2. How do I relate to my colleagues—on the College of Teachers or the faculty—in connection with this fundamental question? Can we arrive at a consensus out of our joint anthroposophical striving?

3. What are the consequences, both overt and underlying, in relation to our tasks with the children?

What Is My Relationship to the Cosmic Christ?

Let us begin with an intimate self-examination which can take the form of a working hypothesis. We should avoid jumping to conclusions and trying to arrive at quick, superficial results. What is needed instead is a longer meditative process, placing the following question again and again to ourselves in the depth of our hearts: Assuming that I have a connection with the Christ Impulse, in which of three ways may that have manifested at the "turning point of time?" Do I sense that during the Mystery of Golgotha, I witnessed the events on earth from a cosmic vantage point, in fact, that I was not incarnated at that time but viewed the descent of the Cosmic Christ from spiritual heights downwards towards His embodiment in the man, Jesus of Nazareth, with whom He became united for a period of three years?

A totally different spiritual and human vantage point was given to those souls who were on earth during the Mystery of Golgotha, who might have known one of the disciples, who might have been acquainted with one of the many women or been in the group of seventy who recognized Christ Jesus. Was I one who saw or heard Him?

We are speaking of an incarnation in Palestine in the Roman or Greek world. We recall that the one named Saul, who became Paul, was of Hebrew descent, and had absorbed both the deepest Jewish and Greek traditions, and was a Roman citizen as well.

So, being a contemporary has to be considered on a wide scale. After the Resurrection, the disciples themselves traveled widely: St. James the Elder to Spain, St. Thomas to India, St. Andrew to Russia, and so forth. The Evangelists also journeyed extensively: St. Mark died in Egypt, St. Luke accompanied St. Paul on his many travels across the lands around the Mediterranean. St. John, as did Peter and Paul, visited Rome and returned via Patmos, a Greek island, to Ephesus which at that time was a Greek colony.

The question that I should ask myself is: Did I, in some way, witness these events, or while in incarnation on earth did I hear someone speak who was a witness?

The third possibility that should be envisaged is whether we belong to those Irish, Hibernian people who, still endowed with a natural clairvoyance, witnessed from a great distance the descent of Christ through the weaving elements of fire, air, water, and earth. An echo of this is found in the legends of St. Bridget and later in the Celtic Irish saints. One might say that this stream has a pagan, pantheistic quality, yet is cosmically Christian in its essence.

A meditative consideration of these three streams can fill our hearts and minds, even if we do not immediately perceive our own specific relationship, and lead to immense tolerance for the varied ways in which the Christ

Impulse can be experienced. Consider for a moment how different it might have been to experience the Christ's descent from a cosmic vantage point, or to have a connection with Him on earth, from beholding His approach to the earth from the region of the Celtic mystery stream thousands of miles away.

What I have attempted to describe above is based on the fact that Rudolf Steiner urged us as members of the Anthroposophical Society, shortly after the re-forging of the Society in 1923/24, to attempt seriously to identify the karmic stream to which we belong. This is delineated by Rudolf Steiner, to begin with, in lectures given in Dornach in 1924, *Karmic Relationships, Volume 3*. The theme is elaborated in subsequent lectures given in Holland and England. It appears that those souls described by Rudolf Steiner as "Platonic" were mainly in incarnation during the Mystery of Golgotha, whereas those characterized as Aristotelian beheld the events of Golgotha in the spiritual world, between death and rebirth.

It is hoped that the relevance of this process can be appreciated, for it represents a demand of our time in order to face the future with greater consciousness. Yet, it is not only a matter for the individual teacher. We have to consider that the children entrusted to our care—to the extent that they, too, belong to one of these three streams—will, in the course of their development at school, manifest quite different characteristics in relation to the central Christ event.

How Do I Relate to My Colleagues?

When working together with colleagues at the level of membership in a College of Teachers (or faculty), we readily become aware that our connections are not simply a coincidence. In a variety of ways—and it is always interesting to examine these—we were brought together in order to work and create the best possible conditions for the education of the children in our care.

We are also aware of the many difficulties and obstacles that impede a harmonious personal interplay, fruitful for the task in hand. This is in no small measure due to the fact that we are attempting, out of Spiritual Science, to shape forms of cooperation which are still in their infancy.

There is no doubt that Anthroposophy, with its emphasis on a path of inner development, can provide us, if it is steadily—and with goodwill and tolerance—practiced over the years, with considerable assistance. The very fact that we are called upon as teachers to work together without there being a school principal marks a totally new social departure. We should reflect on what Rudolf Steiner meant when he said that the leadership should be "republican and not democratic." This implies that each member of the College of Teachers has been given a specific mandate of responsibility over and above the teaching position that he or she fulfills.

In establishing this process and learning to work together, we find that "where we come from" plays no small part. In some Waldorf schools fine steps have been made by sharing biographies. This in itself can work positively in developing tolerance and understanding for what the other colleague has faced, what his or her trials in life have been.

This process could be further developed by asking ourselves—and finding ways of sharing this with colleagues—how we came to Anthroposophy. What paths have led us to recognize the renewal of the Mysteries inaugurated by Steiner and our wish to tread them? Naturally we will find that our karmic threads may have been very different: One colleague might have found in Anthroposophy a way of connecting in a totally non-denominational manner with the Christ Impulse; another may have taken to the cosmology of Spiritual Science; yet another might have been deeply touched by the renewal of a pantheism (a more Celtic approach) related to the Cosmic Christ Impulse. Some have come to Anthroposophy out of a strong previous connection with a Buddhistic or Oriental stream.

We could even ask whether we feel a stronger relationship with the cosmic Michael stream which embraces those who were in the spiritual world during the Mystery of Golgotha, or whether we sense a stronger relationship with those belonging to the earthly Michael stream encompassing those souls who were in incarnation during the Christ event.

It is important to clarify our spiritual origins and then to bring to consciousness what we have been able to make of them. The essence of Anthroposophy is that it unites, in our age, very many diverse spiritual streams. Time and effort should be spent on such examination, certainly not for its own sake, but in order to serve our task more effectively. If indeed there are karmic differences, we should learn to recognize them and to feel that the fullness of the spectrum, like the various colors of the rainbow, is an asset rather than a hindrance.

Here the "Imagination for the Teachers," as given by Rudolf Steiner, can provide us with strong daily quickening of the ideals of our working together. (Details can be found in the recently published book, *Towards the Deepening of Waldorf Education/*) Let it suffice to say that untold strength can be received from picturing in a circle the Angel behind each colleague. Courage is provided through the strength of each, fashioning a vessel by means of which the archangelic presence can be bestowed. Then the "Light" of the Archai realm can be received.

It is my profound conviction that if more time were spent on sharing our karmic connections in a mood of understanding, tolerance, and mutual appreciation, our pedagogical and "business" meetings could be shortened considerably and also leave us active and refreshed rather than, as is unfortunately often the case, tired and depressed. The question really is, whether or not we feel that such basic spiritual work is worth doing in order to heal the many tragic situations that our Waldorf movement is subject to.

What Are the Consequences for the Students in Our Care?

Rudolf Steiner emphasized in a number of lectures that one of the first requirements on the part of the teacher is to take the "unborn-ness" or the spiritual prenatal condition of the human being seriously. We should ask ourselves—and this can become an important regular meditation: What were the characteristics, the particular qualities of the souls before birth when they were guided by the Hierarchies on the way down to embodiment?

In learning to understand a child, it is important to consider—in addition to hereditary factors, which include race, ethnic background, and the biological strands supplied by father and mother—what the soul has brought with it out of supersensible realms. If we deepen this line of thought, we shall take into account not only the prenatal "gesture," but also the spiritual origins as they manifested themselves in previous incarnations. In other words, just as we have applied certain questions regarding our own spiritual origins, we should without jumping to quick conclusions also consider to which spiritual streams our students belonged.

Most probably every experienced class teacher and history specialist in the high school will find that one student, for example, was fascinated by ancient Egypt, another by ancient Greece, yet a third by the lofty, ancient Oriental traditions, which might well indicate—though not necessarily conclusively—that a particular soul recalled something of a previous connection with one or another civilization. A kind of memory feeling was awakened through studying this or that civilization.

But a further dimension should be added. In the many descriptions that Rudolf Steiner gave us regarding the nature of a Waldorf teacher, he pointed to one requirement that may be considered as exceedingly difficult to fulfill. He spoke of the fact that we should consider what we do in education as a continuation of the work of the Hierarchies.

This, to begin with, might appear so lofty and so

remote that we might set it aside and regard it as an impulse that can only be fulfilled at some later time in human evolution when new faculties of spiritual insight will have been developed. But this would be to bypass a most important task that should already be attempted in our time.

Rudolf Steiner pointed out again and again the importance of the first three years in the child's development. In fact, learning to walk, to speak, and to think marks the leitmotif for the whole of life because everything that we do thereafter can be regarded as complex variations on the theme of doing (acting), speaking (relating to one another), and thinking (the sphere of consciousness).

But to whom do we owe these three remarkable gifts that are implanted in our first years? The activity of learning to stand upright and to walk is the gift of the Archai; the gift of speech, of learning to communicate with one another through the word (in different languages) we owe to the impulse of the Archangels; the emergence of the power to think and be conscious of self has been bestowed on us by the Angels. The lofty activity of the Third Hierarchy is active at the very outset of our incarnation after we have descended from the spiritual world. Their activity, of course, does not end with the third year of babyhood, but continues long after in the most complex of weavings.

But when we reflect on the nature of the Hierarchies, we shall find that the Christ Himself as the Son is constantly working through each of them. That is how we can begin to understand what Rudolf Steiner meant when he spoke of the fact that the Christ is especially active in the first three years of the child. It also accounts for the feelings of love and wonder that arise in our hearts in the presence of babies.

We learn to walk in order to find what will become our path in life: "I am the way." Through learning to speak, we are uniting ourselves with "I am the truth." Through the emergence, the lighting up of thinking, we are establishing our relationship with "I am the life." These three "I am" words of the Christ can be expanded as three themes for the totality of our life on earth. Here education plays a central part: Can I as a teacher help the students to enliven their thinking and imagination? Can I guide them to find the truth in the various life situations that they will have to face? Can I assist and support them in finding their path and goal in life? The above thoughts can lead us to a profound inner conviction that in this pedagogical process the Christ Being working through the Hierarchies can accompany us in our everyday task.

We should remember that whatever differences we may experience as colleagues (owing to the past mystery streams to which we belonged), Anthroposophy now offers a finely tuned instrument for harmonizing these various tendencies. This is primarily so because from 1910 on Rudolf Steiner proclaimed the reappearance of the Christ, not in a physical form but now as a supersensible Being who will be experienced more and more for an increasing number of individuals on the etheric plane within the life mantle of the earth. Inherent in anthroposophical striving is the longing to unite oneself with this momentous reality.

Christ in our time is truly reappearing—and that is the

sense of the Second Coming—as the Comforter who brings the Spirit of Truth. But, of course, since we live in an age of freedom, it is for each one of us to strive, step by step, towards this reality and find like-minded colleagues who wish to join us in that search. In this connection, a single sentence in a lecture Rudolf Steiner gave in Vienna on 11 June, 1922, can be used as a potent meditation:

> Anthroposophy seeks in every detail to be a striving towards the permeation of the Christ Impulse in the world.

Chapter VII

The Structure of the Foundation Stone Meditation

The longer one concerns oneself with the Foundation Stone Meditation, the more one discovers that this mantram, given by Rudolf Steiner in 1923/1924, is both fruit and seed. No other meditation embodies so fully the content of Anthroposophy. It represents the mature fruit of a gradual development that spanned twenty-one years. Yet it is also a seed for the unfolding of new capacities that lie dormant within the human soul. Given originally to some eight hundred members of the Society who had gathered for a Christmas conference, it marks the beginning of the New Mysteries. The Foundation Stone Meditation is intended to reach, stage by stage, the whole of humanity. It reveals in the most succinct form possible the human being's relation to our threefold nature and to the macrocosmic Trinity. It also contains a ladder of growth that enables the striving human soul by dint of inner effort step by step to partake consciously in the workings of the Hierarchies.

Let us briefly recall the basic form of this monumental meditation. It is composed of four panels, the first three of which open with the call to the "Soul of the Human Being" and closing with the hope that human beings may hear what the elemental world in East, West, North, and South has already heard. Let us now turn to the first panel which deals with the past.

The Foundation Stone for Teachers:
Panel One

Soul of Man!
Thou livest in the Limbs
Which bear thee through the world of Space
Into the ocean-being of the Spirit.
Practice *Spirit-recollection*
In depths of soul,
Where in the wielding
World-Creator-Life
Thine own I
Comes to being
Within the I of God.
Then in the All-World-Being of Man
Thou wilt truly *live.*

*   *   *

For the Father-Spirit of the Heights holds sway
In Depths of Worlds begetting Life.
Spirits of Strength,
Seraphim, Cherubim, Thrones!
Let this ring out from the Heights
And in the Depths be echoed,
Speaking:
From God, Mankind has Being.
Ex Deo nascimur.

*   *   *

The Elemental Spirits hear it
In East and West and North and South:
May human beings hear it!

Our teaching day has come to an end, and, after due relaxation, we have to set about preparing tomorrow's lesson, but before this we have to reflect, to remember what we have done. What is often referred to as "meditating upon the children" can take many different forms: recalling how the students were dressed, how they behaved, who was present, who was absent. What was the general mood of the class? How did they respond to what you brought? Did you feel that what you had prepared was received as you had hoped it would be? It is important in this process to visualize the children individually as clearly as possible. Going over the lesson in a backward order can strengthen the process.

Perhaps we should attempt to go further in this activity of spirit-remembering. Do we have a clear picture of the past of each child, and can we begin to surmise the particular configuration that influenced each soul before birth? What talents, gifts, but also shortcomings did each child bring with him or her, over and above the heredity factors and the present environment? Such "recalling" might also lead to envisioning a previous incarnation and might throw light on the social configuration of the class; for instance, why certain children relate to others in a particular way, in strong friendships or with obvious animosity. Here again, meditating on the first part of the Foundation Stone can enhance our sensitivity.

Let us now consider this first panel in greater detail. We discover how the soul of the human being lives in the limbs which is the source of our karma. In fact, "spirit recollection" is an essential exercise for discovering the weavings of karma. This holds the riddle of how we are connected with one another from previous earth lives and the mystery of the encounters in our present existence. "Spiritual recollection" is given as the path to learning to "live truly," and it requires the power of intuition.

The second part of the first panel shows how this is possible because of the working of the "Father Spirit of the Heights," with the active participation of the First Hierarchy: the Seraphim, the Spirits of Love; the Cherubim, the Spirits of Harmony; and the Thrones, the Spirits of Will.

This leads us to an experience of *"Ex Deo nascimur"* (Out of God we are born). We recall how Rudolf Steiner emphasized that as teachers we should, in the modern Age of Light, place greater emphasis on "unborn-ness" than on "immortality." We can thus see that the first panel can quicken our sense of memory and recollection which is essential in our daily inner work if we are to serve the children in our care in a harmonious way.

Panel Two

Let us now turn to the second panel which divides in two parts: a microcosmic aspect is followed by a macrocosmic one.

> Soul of Man!
> Thou livest in the beat of Heart and Lung
> Which leads thee through the rhythmic tides of
> > Time
> Into the feeling of thine own Soul-being.
> Practice *Spirit-mindfulness*
> In balance of the soul,
> Where the surging
> Deeds of World's Becoming
> Do thine own I
> Unite
> Unto the I of the World.
> Then 'mid the weaving of the Soul of Man
> Thou wilt truly *feel*.

The above first part of the second panel speaks to us strongly as teachers. It addresses the heart, and whatever we seek to convey to the children in our care needs to have this heartfelt quality which embraces a strong rhythmical element. We need to gauge how much time is spent each day on some topic of our work. Little by little we learn not to rush and yet also not to linger unduly, to repeat but in such a way that each repetition contains something new. Story-telling teaches us to pace the events rightly so that the children can participate not only in the content but also in their breathing.

It may be important to contemplate the feeling element of "heart and lung" in our preparation. We attempt to unite our I "with the I of the World." We discover little by little that we need to "feel truly." It does not come of itself but requires as much practice as mastering a musical instrument. The practice here required is: "Practice Spirit-mindfulness (or awareness) / In balance of the Soul." The original German has the word *Besinnen* which contains the word for the senses, *Sinne*, and the contemplative prefix *be-* which suggests an inwardness.

In the Middle Ages we find the expression *"Sinnen und Minnen"*—which could be rendered in English as "an active, loving day-dreaming" very much connected with the heart. We might say a poetic quality which need not be vague and by means of which we can approach the deep mysteries of nature and the feeling soul.

But the second part of the meditation reveals to us the full macrocosmic import of learning to "feel truly."

For the Christ-Will in the encircling Round
      holds sway
In the Rhythms of the Worlds, blessing the
      Soul.
Spirits of Light,
Kyriotetes, Dynamis, Exusiai!
Let this be fired from the East
And through the West be formed
Speaking:
      In Christ, Death becomes Life.
      In Christo morimur

*   *   *

The Elemental Spirits hear it
In East and West and North and South:
May human beings hear it!

We would be unable to achieve true feeling through the activity of "spirit-mindfulness" had the Christ Being Himself not implanted this very quality in us with the co-operation of the Beings of the Second Hierarchy, the Spirits of Wisdom, of Movement, and of Form.

In our daily work as teachers we must learn to become ever more aware and attentive to the children: their gestures, their ways of speech, their countenance, their joy and sorrow, the way they move. All these are indications of the deeper nature of the children, what they bring with them in this incarnation out of a prenatal life or a former incarnation.

"Practicing spirit-mindfulness" can help us to enter more deeply into the karmic mystery that each child brings with him or her. It starts as a feeling which might then be brought into clear consciousness.

We should live with the question: Where do our

students come from? What is the origin of their gifts and aptitudes, and of their shortcomings? Meditation on the second panel will enable us, through the Christ, to penetrate lovingly and sensitively into this domain.

Whereas the first panel deals principally with the past, the second panel deals with the present, the here and now. The presence of the Christ in the "encircling round," in what weaves from heart to heart (in the horizontal plane from each to each) is here emphasized. This is the social dimension of the Foundation Stone.

Panel Three

Let us now turn to the third panel which again is in two parts. The first addresses the microcosmic nature of the human being; the second, the macrocosmic aspect in relation to the Hierarchies.

> Soul of Man!
> Thou livest in the resting Head
> Which from the ground of the Eternal
> Opens to thee the Thoughts of Worlds.
> Practice *Spirit-vision*
> In quietness of Thought,
> Where the eternal aims of Gods
> World-Being's Light
> On thine own I
> Bestow
> For thy free Willing.
> Then from the ground of the Spirit in Man
> Thou wilt truly *think*.
>
> *   *   *
>
> For the Spirit's Universal Thoughts hold sway
> In the Being of all Worlds, craving for Light.

95

Spirits of Soul,
Archai, Archangeloi, Angeloi!
Let this be prayed in the Depths
And from the Heights be answered,
Speaking:
> In the Spirit's Universal Thoughts, the
> Soul awakens.
> *Per Spiritum Sanctum reviviscimus.*

*   *   *

The Elemental Spirits hear it
In East and West and North and South:
May human beings hear it!

We are now led to contemplate the future, the "ground of the eternal," and are called upon to develop "spirit-vision," in some translations called "spirit-beholding." This exercise, too, is of great importance for the teacher and requires imagination. We have to prepare our lessons for tomorrow, for next week, for next month, and we need to grapple constantly with the riddle: How can we do this best for the unfolding of the children? How can we find a middle ground among presentation, dialogue, and general participation? On which student should I call tomorrow or next week? How can I find a balance between the artistic and the academic, between teaching the skills and quickening the imagination? What should I bring to the class in order perhaps to heal a particular social wound that has occurred between the children?

These and many other such questions require an active picturing of the future. In a larger context, the teacher should be able to imagine correctly how this or that student will develop in ten or twenty years. One might even say that we should cultivate a "prophetic sense," which is so necessary because we are in fact educating for the future when hopefully the child will be able to face life as a self-reliant adult. (It is worth looking at Emerson's essay on self-reliance which to my mind captures one of the finest traits in the American character.) But perhaps, surprisingly enough, this envisioning, this "spirit-beholding" or "spirit-vision" can lead ultimately to "think truly;" in other words, in accordance with the eternal processes of the world.

Looking at the second part of the third panel, it becomes clear that this capacity would not be possible without the fact that the "Spirit's Universal Thoughts hold sway." This points directly to the working of the Holy Spirit, of the Sophia, through the Third Hierarchy of Archai, Archangeloi, and Angeloi. It is summarized in the Latin words which can be meditated upon separately: *"Per Spiritum Sanctum reviviscimus,"* meaning "Through the Holy Spirit we are resurrected."

This of course raises a very fundamental question. If indeed we are predetermined to accomplish certain tasks in the future, where is freedom? Steiner grappled with the question again and again, and *The Philosophy of Freedom* (also entitled *The Philosophy of Spiritual Activity*) offers a fundamental starting point. Freedom and necessity are constantly interplaying. Necessity might be compared to a blueprint. Whether the house will actually be built or not depends on us, and between the plan and the final construction endless variations are still possible. We are not free in an absolute sense. Freedom is a process which actually begins in the sphere of living thinking and will only be ultimately attained in the course of time.

Bringing it in connection with child development, we might say that from the very beginning the child is destined to unfold in a particular way in accordance with his talents, gifts, shortcomings, and obstacles, but how he will develop in time depends largely on the extent to which he develops his own freedom. Nevertheless, the teacher should attempt to sense what this child could become. Education is concerned with bringing forth to the best of our ability what lives as potential in each student.

Panel Four

Let us now turn to the fourth panel which is so different in character from the first three. A tremendous statement regarding the "turning point of time," when the Christ entered the stream of evolution, is followed in the second part by a prayer which is community-forming.

So far, in the first three panels, there has been no explicit mention of the community of human beings on earth. The emphasis has been on the individual and how he or she can make a connection with the Hierarchies. Here in the fourth panel it is very different, also in mood. The second part of the panel points to the need for our active participation.

> At the turning point of Time
> The Spirit-Light of the World
> Entered the stream of earthly Being.
> Darkness of Night
> Had held its sway;
> Day-radiant Light
> Poured into the souls of men;
> Light that gives Warmth
> To simple Shepherds' Hearts,
> Light that enlightens
> The wise Heads of Kings.

*   *   *

O Light Divine,
O Sun of Christ!
Warm Thou
Our Hearts,
Enlighten Thou
Our Heads,
That good may become
What from our Hearts we would found
And from our Heads direct
With single purpose.

In the first part we hear how the light gives "warmth to simple shepherds' hearts" and how "light enlightens the wise heads of kings." We are introduced to two very different streams of human beings: the simplicity of the shepherd tending his sheep, an activity which furthers the natural course of events; and the kings, imbued with insight, who rule their kingdoms in a wise way. These ideal images—the simple, loving shepherd and the wise, enlightened king—symbolically express the contrast between heart and head. It can be useful to ask ourselves in this matter: Do we owe more in our attitude towards life to the shepherd or to the royal stream? Are we more people of the heart or of the head? Do we function better at the level of feelings or more readily out of the concept of the mind?

In the second part of the fourth panel, in the form of a prayer, the uniting of both is sought. We need to "warm our hearts" and "enlighten our heads" because only then can the good be done. But here clearly the "we" and the "our" are emphasized. In other words, we are called to community.

If one is not familiar with the Foundation Stone Meditation, one could well begin by practicing the fourth panel, for it embodies the essence of the New Mysteries initiated by Rudolf Steiner. One of the characteristics of the Old Mysteries was that one had to wait until one was chosen. It was the hierophant who determined who the neophyte would be. The character of the New Mysteries is the very opposite: The individual has to learn to ask the question, to come forward out of his or her own initiative. We need to make the choice ourselves and then set out on a path of inner development.

The prayer-like, meditative form of the final part of the Foundation Stone Meditation, if practiced regularly, will result in the gradual harmonization of thinking, feeling, and willing, the three soul forces of the human being.

One might also take up working on a daily basis with the rhythms of the Foundation Stone as given in the book by Rudolf Steiner entitled *The Foundation Stone*. The whole of the meditation was given on Christmas Day, Tuesday, 25 December, 1923. On subsequent days, starting on a Wednesday, Rudolf Steiner gave a rhythm (that is, a few lines taken from the whole) appropriate for each day of the week. By practicing these rhythms in accordance with the days of the week, one finds that from Wednesday to Tuesday one has actually covered the four panels.

Conclusion

Summary

In summarizing, one might say that to practice spirit-recollection leads into the past, clarifying, shedding light on the events of our life. If pursued far enough, it leads to the crossing of the portal of birth, into our own prenatal existence, into the weaving of our "I" with the Hierarchies in shaping the resolves of our incarnation that was to come. We are gradually led to the experience of the supersensible Michael School and Michael Ritual in which we partook with others preparing for the future. Now we can begin to "live truly," for we have discovered the *"Ex Deo nascimur"* —how out of God we have been born.

To practice spirit-awareness leads contemplatively into the present moment where the Christ-weaving is perceived in the web of destiny that is woven from one to another. Again and again we strive to meet the Christ as "Lord of Karma," strengthening the soul so that we may come to "feel truly." This path leads constantly through dying to new life—*"In Christo morimur"*—we die in Christ so that we may have new life.

To practice spirit-beholding leads prophetically into the future, for now tasks are revealed to us through the resurrected Spirit, the tasks that are to be accomplished on earth quickened by the Sophia in true thinking—*"Per Spiritum Sanctum reviviscimus"*—through the Holy Spirit we are resurrected.

The "ABC" of the Teacher

It has been emphasized that much depends on the inner attitude of the teacher. This of course in no way takes away from the outer preparation which is essential, but we may not always be aware of the fruits that can grow out of a regular meditative practice. It need not even take very long; five minutes in the morning and perhaps ten minutes in the evening on a daily basis can yield remarkable results.

Rudolf Steiner gave three words, known as the "ABC," to characterize the attitude of the teacher: Devotion, Protective Feeling, and Enthusiasm. Each of these is accompanied by a eurythmic gesture.

Devotion—arms folded over the chest in reverence

Protective Feeling—half of a "B" gesture with the right arm

Enthusiasm—the right arm stretched upwards— "E" gesture

What can be meant? Devotion is to be cultivated for what the child brings as the gift of his or her own individuality out of the prenatal life. No child is a *tabula rasa* or "unwritten sheet," but brings with it—in the imagery of Wordsworth—"clouds of glory." These gifts and talents come as the essence of the child's individuality and need to be received with devotion and reverence. We teachers and parents should bear in mind that the child may be far more "advanced" than we ourselves. And it is indeed helpful to remind ourselves that we need not be a genius in order to teach a genius. Our task is to "bring forth" out of the child—a task which reflects the profound meaning of the word education.

But what of a protective feeling? Children need the protection of adults at different stages in their development. Only a mistaken form of bringing up children advocates that we should let a six- or seven-year-old share the problems of our adult life. The youngster needs to be carefully protected until the time in adolescence when he or she can begin to understand in a wider context what is occurring. But even so, adolescents should not be left without judicious protection which should be in tune with their age. Many of the deep social problems experienced today could be remedied if parents and teachers, through their own striving for values, were able to protect the youngsters in a wise way. Temptations that drag the human being down beneath his dignity abound at every turn. Much depends on parents and teachers helping young people learn to cope with drugs, alcohol, and various forms of permissiveness. In actual fact, they long for appropriate guidance.

Enthusiasm is a remarkable word. As in French, in English it contains *theo* which means "god." The equivalent German word *Begeisterung* has *Geist* in it which signifies "spirit." We need to learn to teach out of enthusiasm. Whatever we do with the children throughout the grades must be filled with spirit and a sense of the divine. We live in a time of appalling nihilism when values are being trampled underfoot. For many young people all over the world a hopelessness and despair have set in. But fundamentally, every child, however difficult the circumstances, brings a sun-filled quality into life. Hope and liveliness are the themes of early childhood. All too often the darkening clouds gather and the youngster, filled with despair, faces the abyss of his or her own being and the dark circumstances of life around.

It is up to us as teachers and parents to bring forces of enthusiasm so that the youngster can sense that his or her innate spark of idealism is indeed something real that can be kindled. Here again it is a matter of attitude. It depends on how we teach. What faculties emerge from such disciplines as history and geography? What untold treasures can be unlocked through mathematics and music? It lies more in the "how" than the "what." A striving teacher can renew the spark of enthusiasm for his or her students again and again and thereby enkindle them to strive to find forces within to overcome obstacles.

Final Guidelines for the Teacher

In conclusion, we will turn to the four precepts that, in a lecture on 5 September, 1919, Rudolf Steiner presented to the twelve original teachers of the first Waldorf school in Stuttgart, Germany (cf. *Practical Advice to Teachers*, Anthroposophic Press, Hudson, NY). The teachers were finishing a short, intensive period of training and were about to start teaching. These precepts may also be considered profound meditative sentences.

1. The teacher must be a person of initiative in everything that he or she undertakes, great or small.

2. The teacher should be one who is interested in the being of the whole world and of humanity.

3. The teacher must be one who never makes a compromise in heart or mind with what is untrue.

4. The teacher must never get stale or grow sour, but cherish a mood of soul that is fresh and healthy.

Today in many parts of the world, education has lost a sense of true values and an understanding of the real needs of children. For Rudolf Steiner the task of the Waldorf teacher is to contribute to the healing of modern educational life. These four precepts, as valid today as they were seven decades ago, indicate the high ideal towards which the Waldorf teacher is called to strive so that this task can be fulfilled.

R. M. Querido
Boulder, Colorado
Holy Nights, January 1995

By the same author:

Questions and Answers on Reincarnation and Karma

Creativity in Education

Behold, I Make All Things New
Toward a World Pentecost

The Wonder of Childhood
Stepping into Life

The Mystery of the Holy Grail
A Modern Path of Initiation

The Golden Age of Chartres
The Teachings of a Mystery School
and the Eternal Feminine